Thomas Day

Reflexions upon the present state of England and the independence of America

Thomas Day

Reflexions upon the present state of England and the independence of America

ISBN/EAN: 9783337223939

Hergestellt in Europa, USA, Kanada, Australien, Japan

Cover: Foto ©ninafisch / pixelio.de

Weitere Bücher finden Sie auf **www.hansebooks.com**

REFLEXIONS

UPON THE

PRESENT STATE OF ENGLAND,

AND THE

INDEPENDENCE of AMERICA.

By THOMAS DAY, Esq;

Vedransi sanguinosi battaglie; inauditi assedii; spaventevoli sacchi, incendii, e rovini; successi maritimi, che d'atrocitá non cederanno á terrestri; e non meno atrocemente poi trasportate l'armi da vicini mari d'Europa ne' piu remoti dell' Indie. Uscirà fra l'armi qualche volta ancora il negolio; e frà l'insano strepito della guerra, il desiderio natural della pace Contuttocio prevaleranno poi sempre le rovine, le morti, e le stragi per ogni Cato. *Bentivoglio della guerra di fiandra.*

Our late delusions have much exceeded any thing known in history, not even excepting those of the crusades. For, I suppose, there is no mathematical, still less an arithmetical demonstration, that the road to the Holy Land, was not the road to Paradise, as there is, that the endless encrease of national debts is the direct road to national ruin.—So egregious indeed has been our folly, that we have even lost all title to compassion, in the numberless calamities that are waiting us.

Hume's History of England: Vol. 5. P. 475.

LONDON:

Printed for J. STOCKDALE, opposite Burlington House, Piccadilly, 1782.

ADVERTISEMENT,

THE beginning of this essay was published some weeks past in the London Courant. Reasons of a private nature prevented its continuance at that time; but the importance of the subject, and the critical situation of this country, induced the author to finish it and offer it to the public in the form of a pamphlet. The haste with which it was written, and the necessity of its immediate publication, may perhaps prove some apology for any defects that may be found in the style, method, or arrangement.

ESSAY, &c.

ENGLAND is now placed in the moſt critical ſituation ſhe has ever experienced, ſince ſhe has poſſeſſed that degree of power and pre-eminence which ſhe has held for near a century, amongſt the neighbouring nations. Advanced by a variety of cauſes to that dangerous ſuperiority, which never fails to excite the jealouſy of every other people, that is placed within the ſphere of its attraction, ſhe has not been ſufficiently attentive to prevent by her moderation, that degree of envy which never fails to attend on greatneſs. Added to this, ſhe has miſtaken the very intereſts of her own ambition; and, inſtead of maintaining in perfect vigour thoſe reſources which would have overawed the jealouſy ſhe excited, ſhe has fooliſhly laviſhed them in the moſt wild, unprofitable manner, that ever diſgraced a nation. The Colonies, whoſe importance we now too late acknowledge, appear to have been the immediate causes of her greatness. A country, prolific in all the articles either of necessity or luxury; a climate, varying through every degree of heat and cold; an immense ocean, every where furnished with ports, and inviting the inhabitants to industry and commerce: together with that extent of fertile soil, which seemed to allow the human species liberty to expand for ages yet to come, were such advantages as no period of recorded time has ever seen attached to any other people in the universe. When we add to this, an identity of manners, language, prejudices, religion, nay, of interest itself, it must be confessed that we have no reason to expect a similar phænomenon, unless Providence, by the agency of its most powerful instruments of destruction, should confound the pride of man, and lay the world which we inhabit waste, that the human species might begin their course anew.

But what Nature, which has so widely separated the two countries, had failed to do, what the united force of all the powers of Europe could not have effected, the wild ambition of one part of this nation, assisted by the vanity, blindness, and supineness of the rest, has now perpetrated: America is now divided from the Parent Country, and leaves us nothing but the melancholy consolation of reflecting at leisure on what we have lost; or forming schemes which may at best be visionary,

visionary, and should we fail in wisely managing, the last stake may be fatal.

I will not consume time to enumerate the complicated blessings we have lost, or to execrate the selfish and detestable policy, which grasping at a toy, has thrown away the noblest empire in the universe. I will confine myself to a single point, in the immense chaos of matter which rises before me, and endeavour plainly and distinctly to state the facts which are most necessary to be understood and reasoned from, in our present situation.

England is confessedly in the most critical situation she has ever experienced; with ruined resources, her commerce almost annihilated, her best blood lavished on the detestable schemes of private ambition; her colonies exasperated by persecutions and cruelties, too shocking to be enumerated, and actually emancipated by successful resistance from her dominion; her agriculture, the prop of every society, impaired, and her debts increased almost beyond the possibility of further endurance; she stands singly forth upon the great theatre of the world, unsupported, unassisted, to contend with three powerful nations, almost as much for existence as for command and glory. The rest of Europe keeps aloof, attentive to the mighty contest, and watching every opportunity to promote its respective interests, by the common mischiefs of the combatants; nor is this all,

all, every nation has in turn frowned upon the British advances, and shewed itself inimical to the cause in which we are engaged; nor can I entertain a single doubt, that had it been necessary to the purposes of the American independence, every other people would have successively come forward, and contended with us for the prize. Nature, or Providence, which directs the passions of nations, like those of individuals, to the advancement of their own interests, has, in this case, proposed two of the most alluring objects which can act upon human avarice, or ambition; the abasement of an haughty rival, and the hopes of that immense spoil which the emancipation of America prepares for Europe at large. These dispositions of our neighbours must have been evident, from the very first, to every man who cast the most superficial view upon the state of things, or had the slightest acquaintance with history. The rulers of this country alone appear to have been unacquainted with those truths, which were revealed even to babes and sucklings; they seem to have imagined that France and Spain had forgotten their ancient hatred, their recent wounds; that Holland was become inattentive to her own commercial interests; that every other nation would only see things through the medium of the British Ministry; that every human passion must be hushed, every human interest suspended,

while

while they were permitted to direct the tempests they had raised to the objects of their caprice or hatred. I need not here observe how grosly, how fatally they have been disappointed; the final emancipation of America, the degradation of our naval honour, the loss of almost all our European and Western possessions, is the moderate price which this nation has already paid, for the implicit confidence which the Sovereign has reposed in his faithful and experienced servants. Let us now enquire what are the measures most likely to procure our safety, amidst these complicated distresses.

The original cause of dispute between England and her Colonies, arose from the claim of the British Parliament to levy taxes upon the Americans, exerted in a trifling duty upon tea, imposed in the year 1767. But when, after the violence of the people of Boston, committed upon the teas of the East-India Company in 1773, several acts had passed the British Parliament, each encreasing in severity, which annulled their government, abolished their houses of assembly, deprived them of trial by jury, resigned their lives and property for every, and for no offence, into the hands of Governors nominated by the Crown; and, last of all, absolutely prohibited all commerce between the two nations, and permitted every act of hostility to be exercised upon them:

them: the original cause of opposition was swallowed up in the immediate necessity of yielding to unconditional submission, or of boldly repelling force by force. In consequence, therefore, of these precipitate and violent acts of the English Legislature, which seemed to have no other end than the extirpation of all liberty in America, joined with the mighty preparations made in this country to enforce them, the American Congress made a bold appeal to the first principles of human society, declared themselves independent of a country, which had destined them to slavery and destruction, and invited the rest of Europe to their alliance and assistance. It is evident, that from this moment the original grounds of the quarrel were changed, and the Americans no longer fought to resist, as subjects, the claim of taxation in the British Parliament, but to defend themselves as independent nations, from the attacks of an hostile people, that exerted all its force to reduce them to unconditional servitude. On the contrary, the avowed end and object of the war on the side of England was the reduction of so many independent States to its own dominion. The war which was afterwards begun with France has confessedly the same object; since it was not in consequence of any national dispute with the country, but because it supported the freedom and independence

of

of the American States, that England thought it necessary to begin hostilities; and the treaty of alliance, which was signed between the French Government and the Congress, on the 6th of January, 1778, expressly states in the second article, that, *" The essential and direct end of the present de-* " *fensive* alliance is, to maintain effectually the " liberty, sovereignty, and independence, abso- " lute and unlimited, of the said United States, " as well in matters of government as of com- " merce."

Hence it is plain, that the war which Great-Britain has carried on with the Americans was at the beginning, and has been at every instant of its duration, till the last vote of the House of Commons, strictly speaking, an offensive war; that this offensive war has, in its consequences, embroiled us with France, Spain, and Holland, and still subsists at this moment; since, however respectable may be the opinion of so uncorrupt an House, it will not, I imagine, be pretended, that it bears the authority of a law, in any other case, than that of *disqualifying* the people from chusing their own *representatives*.

After having given these explanations, in order to produce more clearly my ideas upon the subject, I shall reduce the question to a single alternative: Has Great-Britain absolutely resigned her late ambitious views of conquest, or is she still
determined

determined to prosecute the war, till it finally terminate in either her own destruction, or in that of the American States? In the first case, it will be a consideration well deserving the attention not only of the Government, but of the people at large, by what means she may, with the greatest celerity and honour, extricate herself from the fatal labyrinth in which she is involved; in the second, it will *only* be necessary to add thirty millions more to the supplies already voted, to raise sixty or an hundred thousand additional troops; in order, not only to replace those we have lost by sickness, by captivity, by combats, and by desertion, but to enable our Generals to act offensively, with better omens than they have hitherto done. Should we take such vigorous measures as these, notwithstanding the immense difference of the contest, where the overflowing of our goals, the starving remnants of our manufacturers, and wretched German peasants, reluctantly contend with the best disciplined and most warlike troops, assisted, as often as necessary, by the most numerous militia in the world, and this in their own country, where every thing is equally advantageous to them, and hostile to us. Notwithstanding these immense disadvantages, I should think we might fairly hope, by the end of another campaign, for this is already lost, to be in possession of another post; at least, if we add to the

spirited

spirited exertions I have already mentioned, a fleet of forty fail of the line, to prevent the French from pouring in their forces, and turning the balance in a critical moment.

But if these ideas are now reputed chimerical and the experiment of a farther offensive war be rejected with abhorrence, not only by all discerning minds, but by our present Government, supported by a large majority of the people, I apprehend it will be neceffary to enquire, what will prove the moft effectual and speedy means of producing that peace, which is now become so neceffary to our situation.

Those that have done me the honour to read this crude essay with attention, will here, I imagine, anticipate the obvious answer which presents itself. For if the original and continued cause of war, has been the attempt of Great-Britain to subjugate the Independent States of America to her dominion; if farther, Great-Britain, contented with the losses she has sustained, finds herself in no condition to prosecute the claim, and is resolved to desist from an offensive war in America, it will necessarily follow, that the first thing to be done is solemnly to desist from the claim; and in desisting, to acknowledge the independence of America. By this one act, England removes every cause of animosity from between her herself and the American States; by this one act she places herself upon the broad foundation of equity and reason; frees herself from the necessity of garrisoning posts and cities which she cannot hold, is more collected for the defence of herself and her own undoubted rights, and ceases to appear to the rest of Europe in the formidable light of an insolent, unjust, and rapacious conqueror.

It may be here observed, that should we take these steps, should we even abandon New-York and Charles Town, which I should certainly think expedient to be done, the Americans are so involved by the 8th article of the Treaty of Alliance, that they can make no separate peace without the permission of the French.—I answer, that I think all ideas of peace, which are not equitable and general, and which do not extend to all the nations with whom we are at variance, are more calculated to please a party, or serve a Minister, than to extricate the English people from their present complicated distresses.

Since the beginning of the present fatal contest, placed as I am at a distance from the little interests and paltry ambition, which dazzle so many eyes, and turn them aside from the real pursuit of their country's welfare, I have remarked with wonder, the gross falsities and impostures which have so often been current in this metropolis; and I must own, that I have sometimes been

led

led to suspect, that Heaven, in bereaving this country of her former glory, was kindly preparing its inhabitants for the stroke, by depriving them of their senses. For to what causes, short of infatuation, can we attribute the various opinions which have prevailed at different periods of this disastrous contest; that the Americans would never look the British soldiery in the face; that a few regiments would compleat the reduction of that immense continent; that a majority of the Americans were attached to the British government; that the exchanging Philadelphia for Charlestown was the subjugation of America; that Lord Cornwallis with an army of about ten thousand men, could penetrate and subdue all the Southern provinces; that the French would never assist the Americans; and that all the nations of Europe would tamely suffer our maritime tyranny, and the piracies of our privateers? To these might be added, were it necessary to swell the catalogue, many sentiments and observations of Lords and great men of distinguished abilities and importance; such as the opinion of a great Law-lord, that the war in America was a defensive war; the humane declaration of a late American Secretary, that the Americans should be decimated with *more* than Roman severity; and his assertion, that though the Americans had neither money or credit, the English government could raise troops amongst them cheaper than the Congress: to these might be added, the observation of a noble Lord, about six weeks before the surrender at York-town, who, speaking of the Americans, said, with an air of triumph, " *Ils sont au desespoir;* and we are just going to establish the civil government;" of another, who after that surrender affirmed, " that none but British fools would be frightened at the loss of a few thousand troops;" and the opinion of the greatest financier this country has ever seen " that it was necessary to maintain posts in America, for the sake of *commerce.*"

However extravagant these opinions and assertions, when thus crowded together, must appear, I believe there is no man moderately versed in the politics of this nation, during the last ten years, who has not seen them adopted as the principles of our public conduct, or avowed by some of the most distinguished characters in the nation, as necessary to be adopted; nor should I repeat them, in the midst of so important a disquisition, if I did not dread that some new delusion might arise, deprive us of all our present hopes, and plunge us in deeper misery than we have yet experienced. The prejudice which, I must confess, I more particularly dread at present is, that the Americans may be induced to accept of peace, without our acknowledging their independence, and without our comprehending their allies. Whence this opinion
should

should originate, unless from the selfish designs of some men to consult their own avarice or ambition, at the hazard of plunging this country a-new into all the horrors of an inveterate civil war, and from the general inattention of this people to procure genuine information, I own I cannot comprehend. But to those who have only embraced these dangerous opinions, because they are not used to reflect for themselves, I would propose the following considerations: Did not the Americans, when placed out of the English protection by the act, which prohibited all commerce with them as subjects, and permitted every species of hostility to be exercised upon them as enemies, solemnly declare themselves Independent States, by a vote of Congress, dated July 4, 1776? Were all the subsequent successes of the British arms, when Sir William Howe, with an armament capable of carrying terror with it into the most powerful European nation, had landed upon Long Island, defeated all opposition, and seemed to be triumphantly proceeding through the country, capable of determining that body to rescind their vote? Nay, when it was the opinion not only of the majority of the English, but even of the greater part of Europe, that they must fall a prey to the immense exertions which were made against them, did a single State swerve from the general confederacy, or abjure the independence which they had declared? If

If such was the inflexible resolution shewn by the Congress and the American States, when the progress of the British arms on every side seemed to have prevented all future resistance, and to have left them no other alternative, than death, or servitude; when not an European nation had acknowledged their independence, or seemed inclined to share their dangers, by encountering the vengeance of their mighty foe; their resolution and perseverance have not appeared less uniform in that change of fortune which succeeded.

In the Autumn of the year 1777, the brave and unfortunate General Burgoyne surrendered to the American militia at Saratoga, exhibiting a fatal example of the uncertainty of military glories, and the vanity of popular prejudices. About the same time the decided intentions of the French to support the independence of America became apparent; and the abatement of the lofty pretensions of the British Ministry to unconditional submission, produced the famous Conciliatory Bill, which passed March the second, 1778. Those who remembered the frantic exultations of a considerable party of this nation, at the successes which had attended Gen. Howe, in the Autumn of the year 1776, or considered the silent contempt with which the American Petitions had been received at a still earlier period,

riod, could not but deplore the fallen state of their country, which, in a space of little more than two years, had exhibited every degree of insolent despotism, and abject meanness. When the Americans had called upon the British nation by every tie of friendship, interest, and consanguinity, to prevent the wild waste of blood, and happiness which was to ensue; when they stated their complaints with moderation, or petitioned with temper for redress, it was deemed unworthy the dignity of the British Parliament to hear their reasons, consider their intreaties, or even to return an answer. The pretended representatives of a nation, which dares to claim freedom as its right, publicly refused to three millions of men, the licence to state their grievances, or implore redress; and the professors of a religion, promulgated by the lowest orders of men, which breathes an universal spirit of peace and equality, and ordains, that he that is highest shall minister to his brethren even in the most servile offices of life, dared to treat their fellow-creatures, as if they neither owned a common nature, or creator, with themselves. In the same spirit were the commissions framed which accompanied those surer agents of peace, as it was then imagined, the military force. The commissions granted to General Howe, gave him no other power than that of

par-

pardoning all treasons and misprisions of treason, upon proper submission made to him by the Americans. This amazing condescension towards men, who contended, that they were only supporting their own just rights, and who believed, that they had only taken up arms to avoid the last conditions of shame and servitude, was attended with all the effect that its contrivers probably intended. Fresh indignation and hatred on the part of the Americans, who determined rather to perish in one general wreck, than meanly solicit pardon, where they owned no fault, and had themselves complained of injury. Yet notwithstanding those lofty vaunts and arrogance of the British Ministry and Parliament; notwithstanding the repeated victories which had attended our arms, and the utter ruin and despair of the republican party in America, which was propagated and asserted in every corner of this island, we find the second set of commissioners, on the 9th of June, 1778, offering such terms to the rebellious colonies, as were not only infinitely beyond their own desires in 1775, but such as scarcely left to this country the shadow of authority over her revolted children. It may deserve the consideration of those gentlemen, who seem to imagine, that the Americans are to be drawn from their declared independence, from their solemn alliances, from their purposes avowed to
Europe

Europe and all the world, by the firſt gracious overtures of a new Adminiſtration, to conſider what was the declaration of the American Congreſs, dated April 22, 1778, upon the ſubject of this very commiſſion. They declare, " That any man, or body of men, who ſhould preſume to make any ſeparate or partial convention or agreement with Commiſſioners under the Crown of Great-Britain, ſhould be conſidered and treated as enemies to the United States. That the United States could not with propriety, hold any conference or treaty with any Commiſſioners on the part of Great-Britain, unleſs they ſhould, as a preliminary thereto, either withdraw their fleets and armies, or elſe, in poſitive and expreſs terms, acknowledge the independence of the ſaid States.". The anſwer of the Congreſs was exactly conformable to this declaration, and the whole negociation ended in the continuance of the war, and the abandoning of Philadelphia, as a preliminary to the total ſubjugation of America.

If ſuch has been the inflexible ſpirit of America, during every period both of adverſe and proſperous fortune, I would wiſh to know upon what thoſe gentlemen found their opinions, who ſeem to imagine that the Americans will now treat with England, on terms ſhort of independence? —Have our armies been attended with ſuch decisive successes as may inspire this confidence? Have so many nations acceded to our alliance, as may inspire them with doubt and terror? Is it the formidable state of our navy, our finances, or the internal proofs of virtue and consummate abilities which we have displayed to Europe, that support this opinion? Or is it our brilliant successes against the *perfidious* Dutch, a new enemy flung into the preponderating scale, and that master-piece of British valour and policy, the capture of St. Eustatius?

I am the more interested in bringing forward facts like these to the public attention, because I have repeatedly seen the moment of peace and reconciliation flung away, by refusing those concessions which would have purchased them. Had we condescended, in 1775, to consider the American petitions and grant redress; had we, in 1776, instead of pardoning, in the true spirit of a lawyer, treason and misprision of treason, offered them security for the contested points, there can be little doubt that the war would have been either prevented, or speedily concluded. Let the British nation beware how, for the third time, they lose the moment of security which is placed within their power, light up the flame of civil war anew, and expose themselves to suffer, in turn, the evils they have been so long inflicting.

inflicting. Let them remember, that Carthage, the great archetype of England, once covered the seas with fleets, and astonished the world with the rapid augmentation of her opulence and greatness; that she too aimed at distant conquests and dominions, while Hannibal was desolating the fruitful plains of Italy, and thundering at the gates of Rome; but let them also remember, that when the tide of fortune changed, Hannibal was recalled for the defence of Africa, and a single battle decided the fate of Carthage.

As to those who yet flatter themselves that it is in the power of this nation, either to grant or to withhold the independence of America, I must intreat them to consider what it is which constitutes the independence of any country. —Is it not the firm undeviating will of the individuals who compose it not to submit to foreign domination, accompanied with the actual exercise of sovereignty, and the power of defending themselves from all external violence? In all these respects, is not America as actually independent as any nation of Europe, as independent as Great-Britain herself, would she, for an instant, lay aside her habitual arrogance, and consider her own internal situation? For upon what shall we establish our superior claim? Is it upon a short continuance of inauspicious peace, during which the nation has seen almost every post of trust and power filled up by men whom she hated or suspected; the sacred rights of popular election invaded, the streams of justice itself sometimes tainted, sometimes restrained; and every petition of the people treated with undisguised contempt? Is it upon a seven years civil war, into which the most respectable, perhaps the major part of this nation has been reluctantly dragged, and forced to contribute to its continuance by expences almost ruinous to the very existence of their property, like malefactors that are condemned to carry the instruments of their own execution? Is it upon the patience with which this people has borne the destructive burthens of the present war, the wild waste of public property, and the refusal of that moderate redress which Asiatic tyrants would scarcely have refused to Asiatic slaves?——Or is it, lastly, upon that vote of an uncorrupted House of Commons, which establishes the existence of public abuses, in these memorable words, " that the influence of the Crown has been increased, is increasing, and ought to be diminished."

Should any honest minds be offended at the boldness which I use, I must beg them to consider that I do not mention a single circumstance, which has not repeatedly been asserted, and

and reafoned from as fact, by moft of the gentlemen who now compofe our Adminiftration; and I am not willing to lofe that happy moment, which may, perhaps, never return, when I find my own fentiments in perfect union with thofe of the eftablifhed government. If farther apology than this fhould be deemed neceffary, I muft reply, that we have been too long intoxicated with the fumes of our ambition and importance, too little interefted to confider our prefent fituation.—Too long a feries of revolving years has feen us the flaves of impofture and delufion, the prey of idle credulity, and the implicit victims of every interefted fiction. Every fpecies of parliamentary and public information has been fo ftudioufly withheld, that I much doubt if a fingle fact has ever been offered to the people, fince the commencement of the prefent war, upon which we can entirely depend. In the mean time, the good people of this country; that country where the reft of Europe was accuftomed to fend their philofophers, as ancient Greece to Egypt, in order to ftudy morals and legiflation, feems contented with the conviction of its own eftablifhed greatnefs, to have confidered with indifference every circumftance upon which that greatnefs muft depend. Did a new dancer arrive from the opera de Paris, who ftraddled wider,

wider, or capered higher than his noble affociates, you might behold the genuine and undiffembled eagernefs with which the Britifh nobles and fenators confidered the event. His agility, his fhape, his antipoftures, his grimaces, nay, the very ribbands which he wore, and the colour of his breeches, were fcrutinized with all the anxiety of intereft and inveftigation, during fucceffive months. But did an immenfe continent revolt? Was a naval battle loft, although its lofs might fhake the very foundation of our naval and commercial greatnefs? Was a Britifh army captured, or an ifland loft? It was juft whifpered upon the Exchange, repeated at a city dinner, jefted upon by a court Lord, and then configned to eternal oblivion.

But it is now time for the Englifh nation to roufe from that delirium in which it has dreamed of conqueft and dominion, in the midft of thofe luxuries and pleafures which not only incapacitate it to command others, but even to preferve its own liberty. If my countrymen wifely bound their ambition with being the firft dancing and fiddling nation in Europe, it is neceffary to refign thofe fchemes of power and conqueft, which would only ferve to draw their attention from thefe objects: but if fome remains of antient pride, and the memory of paft glories, fhould rufh upon their minds, and ftimulate them to new exertions, they

cannot

cannot too soon or too attentively confider their prefent situation, left thofe exertions, like all the reft, fhould be ineffectual, and only exhauft the fafter their few remaining refources. Nations, like individuals, can only hope to fucceed while they proportion their enterprizes to their force, and wifely aim at poffibilities: that people will never be deferted by fortune, which is not wanting in itfelf, and which endeavours with fortitude and wifdom to atone for former rafhnefs. But violent and injudicious efforts, however they may flatter the public pride, will never alleviate the public diftreffes; they are lefs the fymptoms of health than the agitations of convulfion, which do not portend recovery, but approaching diffolution.

I cannot therefore too ftrongly inculcate upon my countrymen, the neceffity of mixing with that fortitude which is fo requifite in their prefent circumftances, fome portion of that good fenfe for which they were once fo defervedly famous.— This, I cannot help believing, will evince, if properly exerted, the neceffity of chufing one of the alternatives which I have mentioned; either that of profecuting the war againft the Americans, to fubdue them by force, or of granting their independence, and general terms of peace to all the nations we have irritated. Let the inhabitants of this metropolis, that fertile foil, where every feed of prejudice and abfurdity is generally found to

ger-

germinate with the rankeft vegetation, recal for an inftant, their own fenfations in refpect to the rioters of 1780. The outrages of thofe unhappy men were partial, and affected but a fmall number of individuals; yet let them recollect the general confternation and horror which were produced in almoft every mind; and which feemed, for fome confiderable time, to have extinguifhed even national humanity. The ftreets heaped with the dead and dying, during the military fury which raged for fome days uncontrolled; and the yet more awful fpectacles of promifcuous and implacable juftice, ferved only to gratify the ftern refentment of the mildeft people in Europe, and to fill them with filent fatisfaction. The very eyes of the fofter fex, accuftomed to weep for every trivial, for every fictitious woe, feemed to refufe a tear for the numberlefs miferies that furrounded them; fo vaft, fo many are the facrifices which the jealoufy of invaded property demands for the flighteft offence. This recollection, I fhould think, might teach my countrymen to uefs at fome part of the fenfations which muft rankle in the bofoms of the Americans. They have feen their property laid wafte, their towns and cities confumed, their country defolated with all the fury that marks the laft exceffes of war, inflamed by civil hatred; every infult has been offered to their women, every degree of fcorn and inhumanity

nity to thofe who were taken prifoners, and every
fpecies of barbarity to thofe who refifted : even the
favage tribes, whofe manners are fometimes quoted
to exprefs a degree of atrocious cruelty beyond
the corruption of polifhed nations, were not judged
unworthy of the alliance of finging, fiddling,
Frenchified Britain, or agents improper to be em-
ployed in her domeftic quarrels. But it has pleafed
that Providence, to whom the folemn appeal of
both countries has long been made, to reprefs the
arrogance of this country, blaft her ambitious
defigns, and bid her vengeance and her infults
recoil upon her own devoted head; and now, dif-
graced and baffled with fmothered rage and una-
vailing pride, we reluctantly prepared for peace.
Are we yet to learn that the Americans are men;
men that can feel as deeply as ourfelves the fenfe
of injury and injuftice; men that poffefs reafon
and paffions in common with ourfelves, and
haughty minds, ftimulated at once by vengeance
and elevated by fuccefs?—If fo, what is there to
juftify the fond and foolifh prejudice which leads
us to imagine they will, at the firft invitation,
abandon in our favour all the alliances they have
contracted, entail perpetual infamy upon their
rifing name, and ftain with the imputation of
levity and falfehood, all the trophies they have
raifed? Is it the old prejudice, that almoft a
fourth of the whole earth requires the affiftance of a

E.   fmall

small damp island, placed at the distance of many thousand miles, in order to enable it to subsist? Are we yet to learn that America possesses every variety of product which this country could ever boast; all that the warmer suns of Spain and Italy can ripen, with thousand others, denied to the industry of Europe? Or do we believe that the choice and excellence of our manufactures will make them again accept our empire? This reason, though better founded than the last, will be found equally vain; for a more urgent necessity presses us to sell than them to buy, and every nation in Europe is preparing to extract her own advantage from our mistakes; every port is opening to their ships, and every state soliciting their commercial alliance. Or perhaps it may be the blessings of our envied and admired constitution that may soften their stubborn souls; and they may pant for the splendour of a civil list, for the œconomy with which our finances are managed; for the blessings of bishops and hereditary nobles; for the intricate magnificence of our Gothic tenures; for a clergy to decimate their agriculture, without performing in person a single duty of their office; for a navigation act to improve their commerce; and for mysteries of a virtual representation to secure their freedom.

Let us for once be candid, and acknowledge that we have nothing, in our present situation, to allure

allure the Americans to a participation; that men, who have toiled through feven bloody years to eftablifh their right to freedom will haidly throw away, without a motive, the harveft of their toils, and fubmit to wear the yoke which they had broken to pieces; let us allow that Providence, wherever it has given a fertile foil and temperate climate, has intended the human fpecies fhould exift and increafe, without afking the privilege from equals, who are feparate from them by the whole habitable earth, or half the extent of ocean; let us allow that men that poffefs reafon, induftry, and experience, and that have emancipated themfelves from the chains and prejudices of Europe, may provide for their own internal policy, and external defence, without the affiftance of Englifh lawyers or an Englifh Houfe of Commons.

Nor, could the fhadow of a connection, the chimera of a political union, be admitted by the keen-fighted, jealous Americans, can I conceive at prefent any other effects which would arife from it, but new wars, new mifchiefs, and new declarations of independence. Upon what terms, I afk, is it to exift? Is it to be a mere vague, unmeaning, undefinable acknowledgment of dependence, while their provincial governments retain all the attributes of perfect and unlimited fovereignty? Is fuch a paltry fubterfuge worthy to be
propofed

proposed by us, or granted by them? Would it not add ridicule to our disgrace, as if our pride was capable of being soothed with so paltry a concession; as if we chose to derive our titles from what we had lost, and like some of our own noble spendthrifts, to be only pointed out by the estates we had alienated and squandered? but we must, I fear, pay an higher compliment to the great politicians amongst us, who are contending for such a scheme.

They must certainly have a wider reach, and intend to secure something like a constitutional subordination in America, even though they give up the exploded principles of taxation, and permit the infringement of the Act of Navigation. But are we so little acquainted with human nature, as not to see that this would answer no other purpose, than that of keeping alive a continual distrust in the Americans, a continual jealousy of intended encroachment, and would eternally prevent the ancient wounds from closing? From the present Administration I can, indeed, fear nothing, because there is scarcely a man amongst them, that is not personally pledged to the people for the integrity of his intentions, and for the redress of public grievances. But is their continuance eternal? have we not seen premature political death cut off as promising administrations, even in the bloom of sportive infancy?—Alas! who does

not

not know the thousand unforeseen contingencies that may deprive us of the fruits of their labours, and change the present mild, pacific, unoffending spirit of our councils, into gall and rancour?—But how is this subordination to be secured? Is it to be guaranteed by Congress, or is it to be maintained by those *red-coated* citizens, who enforce the execution of civil laws, under the denomination of a military force? In the one case, I fear, left the dependence should be merely nominal, although it produce most of the inconveniences of a real one; in the other, I dread, least the Americans should object to resigning every thing into the hands of military guardians, without overawing them by a superior number of their own militia. In that case, where will be their efficacy?—Or were they nearly balanced, who will insure the continuation of even a month's agreement between high-minded men accustomed to decide every thing by the sword, and inspired with all the animosities which the present contest has breathed into their souls? Should feuds arise, should blood be shed, will their respective nations be unconcerned spectators of the fray? And then the offices of state, are they to be filled up by Congress, by the people of every state, or by the British Minister?—Will the Americans acquiesce in such nominations? Will they suspect no frauds, no influence, no interference of the Treasury, no attempts upon their *Roman* virtue?—Or, should they suspect such practices, however innocent, will haughty souls like theirs tamely acquiesce, in suffering British gold to win its way where British steel has failed? Will they not return with tenfold fury to their beloved Independence, and will not every circumstance I have mentioned be sufficient to dissolve the feeble connection, or kindle the ill-extinguished flames anew?—

But I am reasoning about events, which are so little likely to happen, that they scarcely deserve a moment's consideration; and the two principal divisions of politicians in this country, cannot, without the last inconsistency, admit their probability for an instant. Those who have always asserted, that the Americans have long desired independence, even prior to these unfortunate disputes, can hardly imagine that they will give up the darling object of their intrigues, the very first moment they have obtained it; and those who believe the assertions of the Americans themselves, and the evidence of events, that every step they have taken in this affair, has been suggested and necessitated by the persecutions of this country, will not believe that they will, on a sudden, acquire so much confidence in us, or retain as little in themselves. It is now time for the English to

lay

lay afide their foolifh contempt of men, who are defcended from their own nation, who boaft an equal fhare of all the qualities which have ever diftinguifhed it; and to believe that the Americans no more want ability in their councils, than valour in the field. Let us not then imagine them fo grofsly ignorant of their own fituation and of ours, as to grant to negociations what they have refufed to arms. Let us not imagine them either fo devoid of reafon, or of honour, or fo ignorant of their own effential interes, as to enter into any treaty with us, which would cover them with the imputation of perfidy, and deprive them of the friendfhip and affiftance of the other nations of Europe. Were it even poffible that the great body of the people of America, for there is no virtual reprefentation there, fhould overlook the neceffary confequences of fuch a meafure, let us have a better opinion of the abilities and of the ambition of their leaders, than to imagine that they would fuffer them to accede to fuch propofals, without opening their eyes to all its poffible effects. We did not find them fo eafy to be deceived, or wrought upon, when the conciliatory propofitions of 1778 were fent over; and we muft have a very peculiar view of human nature, if we imagine that fuccefs is likely to render the mind more tractable and humble. Have we ever experienced thefe effects ourfelves?

Let

Let me now be permitted to enquire what are the advantages likely to enfue from a generous avowal of the independence of America. The firſt advantage which I think will ariſe from it, is that of changing the entire nature of the conteſt, and placing Great Britain in a leſs odious point of view to all the neighbouring nations.

When we take a retroſpective view of modern hiſtory, we ſhall find that almoſt every people of Europe has, at ſome period of their exiſtence, been ſeized with the delirium of extending their power by conqueſt; and of theſe bold diſturbers of human peace, that there is ſcarcely one that has not expiated its raſh exertions, by ages of inactivity and weakneſs. Venice, Portugal, and Sweden, have juſt aſtoniſhed the world, like ſhort-lived meteors, by their tranſitory greatneſs: Spain and France have ſcattered terror and diſmay, with the more continued blaze of comets; but both the former and the latter have reſigned their place to England, who, unterrified by paſt experience, ruſhed forward in the ſame mad career, and advanced rapidly to her decline. Europe, that had ſo often ſeen her the patroneſs of liberty, and the generous foe to tyrants, beheld her infatuation with mingled grief and pity, till, rouſed by the ſtrong impulſe of intereſt, or irritated

itated by injuries, the different nations that compose it have either engaged in the contest, or prepared themselves to repel the violence they dreaded, with equal violence. But this jealousy of England, like the causes that have occasioned it, is transitory and easy to be removed. The natural envy that attends a powerful and conquering nation, a . t of moderation in the exercise of that super. v, and the immense spoils which the emanci,. " of America from all commercial restraints o- mises to the different kingdoms of Euro; e, have been the causes that have indisposed them against their ancient friend and ally. It may have been their interest, it may have been their passion, to clip the wings of her inordinate ambition, and to increase their own naval importance, by lowering hers. But the hour of British insolence is past, the measure of her disgrace is full, and it can neither be their interest or their passion that England should be reduced beyond a certain point; still less can it be their aim and object to support the maritime greatness of France and Spain, those ancient and inveterate enemies to the common liberties of Europe.

Let England, therefore, give up the only object which the rest of Europe demands; an object she may yield with magnanimity, but cannot

F   withhold;

withhold; and from that inſtant ſhe will be enabled to make an honourable peace, or, if compelled to carry on the war, the principles and fortune of it will be changed. France has hitherto had the addreſs to cover her ambitious views with the ſpecious ſemblance of moderation; ſhe has ceaſed to be the common invader of all her neighbours, and the diſturber of the general peace; ſhe is become the patroneſs of univerſal liberty, the guardian of public rights, and the diſintereſted championeſs of the diſtreſſed. England, on the contrary, from the unfortunate principles of the war in which ſhe is engaged, and from the headlong ſpirit of revenge with which ſhe has proſecuted it, has loſt the advantage of the ground, and preſented herſelf to the eyes of Europe, too much in the light of a proud, imperious conqueror. So long as ſhe ſuffers the conteſt to be carried on upon its preſent principles, that diſadvantage will remain; and her crafty rival may bereave her of all her moſt valuable poſſeſſions, with the appearance of defiring peace, and only acting upon the defenſive. But let England once deſiſt from thoſe ambitious ſchemes of ſubjugating the Colonies, which have already coſt her ſo much; and offering them the conteſted points, offer to her other enemies an equitable peace; and France, who is the principal of her enemies, will either be compelled to accept it, or to loſe

her

her prefent fituation. Not all the artifices fhe can then ufe, not all her policy, will then prevent her from appearing the aggreffor; and fhe will excite fo much the more jealoufy and fufpicion, as her prefent diffimulation is deeper, and her ambition more carefully concealed.

If we now confider the confederacy which is formed againft us, we fhall find it compofed of the moft difcordant and heterogeneous elements. All the States that conftitute it, vary as much in their refpective interefts, as they do in language, manners, prejudices and government. America with a wifh of which, perhaps fhe is fcarcely fenfible, to be reconciled to the parent ftate, provided England will treat her like a child that is arrived at maturity, and acknowledge her independence, is obliged to treat a nation, of whofe defigns fhe is fecretly fufpicious, with confidence and refpect. France, on the contrary, whofe darling object is to weaken the naval power of England, till it become inferior to her own, is fupporting a rifing empire, of which fhe either is, or fhortly will be jealous. Holland, irritated by the injuries and provocations fhe has received, by the invafion of her commerce, the capture of her fettlements, and the intrigues which fhe fufpects this country to have carried on againft her liberty, is waging a war of defence, of indignation, and of revenge. Spain, who had originally but little inducement to intermeddle, is probably bribed with the hopes of recovering Jamaica and Gibraltar; and without farther confideration, intereſt, or paſſion, is combating to aggrandize an ally, againſt whom ſhe entertains a ſecret and hereditary hatred.—If the view, which I have here preſented, of the intereſt and deſigns of the ſeveral nations with whom we are involved be juſt, it muſt appear probable, that the obſtinacy of England, in proſecuting a war, to ſubjugate the colonies, and her impatience of every obſtacle, have proved the ſtrongeſt bonds of confederacy to her enemies. The æra, therefore, of her deſiſting from this deſtructive claim, whoſe fatal conſequences ſhe has ſufficiently experienced, will be the commencement of diſcord and diſtruſt, amongſt allies, whom accidental, not permanent intereſts have united. France, herſelf, ſhould ſhe be guided by enlightened and extenſive views of her own intereſt, may be contented with the honour and advantages ſhe has gained, and wiſely fear a reverſe; ſhe may perhaps perceive, that the project of deſtroying the public credit, and exhauſting the reſources of England, may, by a continuance of the war, recoil upon her own head; and theſe conſiderations may make her as willing to accept, as we are to offer terms of peace. As to Holland, although the preſent impulſe of paſſion, and the deſire of revenge, may momentarily tranſport her from her natural peaceable bias, there is little doubt

doubt but she will be softened, when she perceives a real and important change in the councils of this country; and that she will soon sicken of a war, where all the advantages will naturally center in her more powerful allies, and where victory, no less than defeat, may be prejudicial to her commercial interests. As to Spain, as no particular interests or passions have led her into the war, so we may not unnaturally imagine that she will be glad to free herself from the dangers and expences which attend it, by seizing the first opportunity of an honourable peace; more especially if any unexpected misfortune should intervene, to abate the pride, which unwonted successes may have raised.

As to the other nations of Europe, I cannot retain a doubt, that they would then find it as politic to reduce the insolence of France, as they now have that of England, and that allies would not be wanting in so just a cause, if necessary. Nor would the advantage be less conspicuous, as to every purpose of internal defence. For every difference of opinion must then be silent, every murmur of discontent and opposition hushed, when the immediate question related only to the common safety of the country. What individual, that bore the name of Englishman, would not feel himself rouzed to every noble exertion? Who would refuse to contribute his property in any required portion, when he was certain it would
be

be applied to national defence, not to the wild purposes of enslaving others, bribing the pretended representatives of his country, or to sustain the luxury of proud unfeeling oppressors?—Who would even withhold his blood, if that blood was necessary to defend his own just rights, and save his country's honor and independence from destruction? Thus, and thus only, would the resources of England be found really inexhaustible; when every scheme of selfish ambition was given up, when principles of justice were substituted to the low intrigues and frauds that have long disgraced her councils, and when the Ministers of the Sovereign, were at length become the friends and patrons of the public liberties.

A very considerable portion of this nation has been long in avowed opposition to public measures; because they believed those measures, with whatever success attended, adverse to the interests and liberties of their country. These men have been reviled with every odious epithet which slander, falsehood, and malice could invent: they have been represented as serpents that were fostered in their country's bosom, while they were watching every opportunity to sting her to the heart. I believe that most of these gentlemen have treated such insinuations with the same contempt that I have felt myself. But it is incumbent on all, that have avowed these principles of opposition, to embrace

embrace the firſt opportunity of proving, that they are animated with as warm a zeal for their country's welfare, and dare as nobly in her juſt defence, as thoſe whoſe vaunts and menaces have been heard the loudeſt. It is alſo incumbent upon them to evince, that their attachment to America, has been the attachment of virtuous citizens, who think the real intereſt of their country can never be promoted by execrable and ſelfiſh ſchemes of enſlaving others; not a guilty preference of America to England. Nor can I doubt, though little inclined to pledge myſelf for the conduct of others, that ſhould the Americans once abandon the juſt grounds of ſelf-defence, and after having been offered the long conteſted independence, and terms of peace which they may accept conſiſtently with their treaties, league with the enemies of Britain for her farther humiliation, that from that inſtant, their warmeſt friends would become their moſt inveterate enemies.

Something remains to be ſaid of the Americans themſelves; and as far as human reaſon may pretend to foreſee the future, theſe are the conſequences which I ſhould think might be expected to ariſe from an acknowledgment of their independence. Perſecuted as they have been by the arms of Britain, ſtruggling at once for liberty and exiſtence, it is no wonder, if every former ſentiment has been ſuſpended, and if affection has

yielded

yielded its place to bitterness and rancour. Still less can we be surprized, if they should have found a friend in every enemy to Britain, and have gladly entered into every alliance that supported them against her vindictive claims. Those, who at the same time that they justified the Americans in the first periods of their resistance to Britain, have blamed them for their declaration of independence, and their treaties with France, seem to possess but little acquaintance with human nature; or even with the necessary consequences of their own principles. If such things exist as human rights, which ought to be the basis of every society, and which, when once invaded, leave mankind at large to consult their own preservation, by following the dictates of reason and experience; it must be granted, that the American independence was not only justifiable, but unavoidable. How could men that had been deliberately placed out of the protection of this country, and devoted to destruction, consider themselves as owing any thing to their destroyer? Or how could that destroyer be considered as the proper guardian of the very rights which she had invaded, after they had been snatched from her oppression, by the bloody operations of the sword? Britain might, indeed, talk of benefits, consanguinity, and gratitude, at the very instant that she was spreading havock and devastation; and attempt to persuade the Americans that

that thefe were only fymptoms of her maternal care and her zeal for conftitutional liberty. But not all the fophiftry of her ableft advocates, the diftinctions of her lawyers, or the pious hypocrify of her churchmen, can be expected to fil·nce the feelings of our nature, or convert the exceffes of irritated pride into the effufions of tendernefs and affection. Thofe that believe tyranny to be the favourite attribute of Divinity, and that Providence had no other end in creating the innumerable millions which people the earth, than to foothe the pride, or employ the vacant moments of its lazy and befotted vicegerents, may be ftartled at every exertion of human liberty. But thofe, that in the human fpecies, behold an animal endowed, indeed, with nobler faculties, and deftined ultimately to an higher end, but agitated and impelled by the fame paffions which govern every other kind, will laugh at the opinion, that there are individuals only born for the fervice of others, or nations that are not to exift without the permiffion of their equals. When they are gravely told, that the Americans muft not make laws for their own government, becaufe they are originally defcended from the Englifh, they will afk, if the courfer that bounds along the mountains of Chili, muft not graze the herbage, or tafte the fpring, without the formal permiffion of his Andelufian brethren? Or whether the patient ox, that flowly breaks the

G fallows

fallows of our western hills, may claim a right to dispose of the immense Savannahs of America? They will ask, if there is any law of Heaven or Nature, more certain, more universal, more obligatory, than that of self-preservation; and whether Great Britain, when she obliged the Americans to draw the sword for their own defence, did not herself wave every other claim, and dissolve every other compact?——If, therefore, the Americans were right in the first moments of their resistance, it will follow, that they were right in every subsequent one; since the same imminent necessity continually impended; since gratitude and persecution, government and hostility, are incompatible terms; and since universal experience has demonstrated, that no human passion is so little to be trusted as disappointed ambition. That necessity, therefore, which made them first take up arms, produced their independence, and their alliance with France; and that independence must incline them to league with every nation that is inimical to Britain, so long as Britain retains the power and the inclination to annoy them. The basis, therefore, of this alliance is mutual dread, and mutual jealousy of this country; and the policy of those who think it is to be dissolved by a continuance of the war, unless we deem ourselves equal to the conquest of both nations, resembles the attempt of the North Wind in the Fable, to

make

make the Traveller lay afide his cloak; the keener blew the blaft, the clofer he wrapt his mantle round him, to defend him from its feverity.

But let Great Britain defift from her chimerical attempts to fubdue a country that is at this moment better prepared for internal defence than herfelf; let her either withdraw her garrifons from the American towns, or ftipulate to withdraw them upon fair and honourable terms; let her above all give every evidence, that under the propofals of reconciliation, fhe conceals no infidious project of renewing a war of conqueft, and it is probable that fhe may unbind the chain, which all her forces would never be fufficient to break. It is evident that from this moment the Americans will ceafe to confider the Englifh people as their foe; that from this moment every former prejudice in their favour will be revived, and every antient affection recur to their minds. Their prohibitory laws will be repealed, their fhips, no longer fettered by the tyrannic influence of navigation laws, will voluntarily find their way to our ports, and their harbours in return will be open to our fleets. The induftry and ingenuity of our manufacturers will again find ample employment, when fo immenfe a market is opened to their exertions. In this fenfe, the colonies will ftill be ours; ours in every rational and enlightened view of intereft, without infringing the rights of nature, or violating the laws of humanity. Every increase of population, or agriculture amongst them, will equally contribute to our advantage, by the increased demand for our commodities; thus will they voluntarily alleviate our burthens, and bear without repining, the enormous weight of the public impositions here. And indeed, if we consider the true interests of this country, we shall find that it is commerce alone which had raised us to our late envied pitch of greatness; and that it is by commerce only that we can hope to preserve some political importance, and the shattered fragments of our empire. We neither possess that vast extent of country, or population, which can fit us to aspire at dominion by conquest. Above all, our insular situation, while it secures us from the sudden irruption of our neighbours, renders them in turn more independent of us. For although the empire of the sea, may in a certain degree command respect by land, yet I cannot recollect a single instance of any country's being conquered by a naval invasion, that possessed even moderate resources, or the common means of self-defence. The Carthagenians, who were destroyed by Scipio, in the third Punic War, constitute no exception; since they were first exhausted by their own imprudent efforts, and afterwards deserted by the other nations of Africa, to whose jealousy the greater part of the Roman success was owing. Still less,

less, can the conquest of the new world by Cortez, in the sixteenth century, be admitted in opposition to the rule; for there, the inequality of arms and discipline operated with an almost irresistible force; yet even that superiority would have been vain, had not the impolitic jealousy of the Tlascalans saved the common destroyer from impending ruin, and first established the Spanish tyranny in Mexico. But as Britain can never look for similar contingencies, so she will be precluded from the dangerous delusion of attempting distant conquests, the instant she properly considers the nature of her own insular situation. Happy indeed would it have been for her, had she perceived this great truth a little earlier. For had she cast even a superficial view upon some of the most important parts of her history, she would have seen enough to sicken her with the very idea of carrying on an offensive war, more especially at such a distance, as must inevitably render courage, policy, and even riches vain, if she had to do with enemies that were not wanting to themselves. What end did all the decisive victories which she formerly gained over the French produce, but new toils, new contests, fresh waste of blood and treasure, and at length her final expulsion from every province which she had ever held? What were the effects in the beginning of the present century, of all the bloody wars about the Spanish succession?

fion? Did they not end, in fpite of all her boafted advantages, in the accumulation of her own debts, and the eftablifhment of the very competitor they were meant to exclude? Have not the fame effects, at a later period, been the uniform confequences of every continental war fhe has waged. And in refpect to the prefent American conteft, did not every difpaffionate perfon foretell the event, or at leaft demonftrate, that whether baffled or victorious, fhe muft fuffer mighty loffes, fuch as fhe might never recover, without the leaft rational hope of advantage. For granting for an inftant, that the firft victories of the Britifh arms had been as decifive as they were fplendid, I cannot help deliberately afferting, that unlefs we had given up all the controverted points at once, and endeavoured to reconcile the irritated minds of the Americans, by reftoring to them all they had loft, the event might have been fomething later, but would have been precifely the fame as at prefent. As to the firft alternative, I leave good men to conjecture the nature of that conftitutional liberty which was intended for the conquered Americans; but I cannot help making fome reflections upon the fecond cafe, becaufe the ideas of conqueft, however fuppreffed by the little checks we have received in our career of victory, do not feem entirely extinguifhed in fome minds. Let us therefore fuppofe that the fame

expence

expence of blood and treasure, which at the end of seven years has placed this country in a worse situation, both as to conquest and defence, than at the beginning, had produced a temporary cessation of hostilities; and that after a certain number of civil and military executions, confiscations of property, &c. &c. his Majesty's peace had been successively proclaimed in all the thirteen provinces of America. May we not suppose, that the same excellent policy which inclined our government to make war, in order to reduce the exuberant spirit of liberty in the colonies to the proper bounds of loyalty and discretion, would have judged it equally expedient to provide for futurity, by modelling their respective governments to that excellent system of constitutional liberty, which is at this day found in Canada? And would not such alterations have probably left that leaven of discontent, which would have made it necessary to maintain a military force amongst the conquered, amounting to at least forty or fifty thousand men, to prevent future insurrections? Must not that military force have been continually increased with the increasing population of America, which is reckoned to double in about twenty years, to prevent its becoming inadequate to it's intended object? And would it have been an easy task to govern eighty, an hundred and sixty thousand men, and the indefinite multiples of that number,

ber, by orders from the War-Office here? Would it have been agreeable to our gentlemen, who with so much true wisdom and sound policy voted the American war, in order to lower their own taxes, to see the land-tax doubled, trippled, &c. in order to pay their military deputies in America? Or, can any one suppose, that the desolations of such a war, as would have subdued all opposition on that continent, would have left the inhabitants any resources to pay such a peace-establishment? As there must have arrived a term, beyond which it was utterly impossible to increase the numbers of our army there, would it not have been at least necessary either to prevent the farther increase of population by an act of our omnipotent Parliament; by destroying a given proportion of all the children that should be born; by selling them as journeymen to the loyal manufacturers of Liverpool, Manchester, &c. or else to relinquish at some given period, the whole American continent, and leave it to that independence which we so much dread? And lastly, would there not have been some danger in the mean time, that all our ambitious neighbours in Europe, would have continually cast an eye to America, as our most vulnerable part; and have requited every real or imaginary offence from us, by entering into leagues with the exasperated colonies, sending them effectual succours to excite new rebellions,

and

and lighting up new wars; till the utter ruin of this country had produced the final emancipation of all its dependencies?

It is not without particular defign, that I have entered into this digreffion; for I have feen my countrymen fo generally elated with the late trifling and accidental fucceffes, and forming to themfelves fuch mighty and chimerical expectations, which feem to embrace no lefs an object than the deftruction of the whole naval forces of all their enemies, that I cannot help trembling for the event. Convinced as I am, that there is no alternative between giving up the independence of America, and feizing the firft opportunity of making a general peace, or of engaging anew in all the horrors and difafters of a war of conqueft, which muft end in the utter ruin of this country, I cannot help attempting to rouze them from their temporary delirium, which is as little allied to real greatnefs as it is to found reafon and policy. For this reafon, I have ftated the confequences, which appear to me inevitable, had even the Britifh arms, in the commencement of the prefent war, been attended with the moft ample and unequivocal fuccefs.—But if we are to confider the fuccefs of Admiral Barrington, as the beginning of a new war, which fome of our politicians have afferted, let the Englifh people confider, while they are yet upon the fhore, the immenfity of that sea on which they are preparing to embark! What deluges of blood must flow, what millions of treasure be consumed, before this country could be brought back to a situation in which she had the smallest hopes of success! As to the united navies of our enemies, are they not confessedly to ours in the proportion of three to two? Have not the French, in every engagement, given such decisive proofs, both of seamanship and courage, as to leave us no pretence to victory, upon equal terms, and frequently scarcely the poor consolation of explaining away a defeat? Have not the Dutch, whom, in spite of British prejudices, I do not hesitate to name a brave and injured nation, given us such unequivocal proofs of cool and inflexible bravery, that we seem ready to shrink from the contest which we had so wantonly provoked? What else did all those public rejoicings mean, upon the bare idea of a separate peace with a people, whom, within scarcely the interval of a year, I have heard reviled with every odious epithet, in every part of this metropolis? I am too sensible, that truths like these, are little calculated to gain me either favour or popularity; and would some abler pen have undertaken the necessary and dangerous task of awakening the public to their own affairs, by telling bold unpalateable truths, I should with pleasure have continued in native unmolested obscurity.—But since no abler advocate has

has chosen to appear, and since some possible good may arise from even these weak endeavours, if they should turn the public attention to the sober discussion of these important points, while all the risk and danger are entirely my own, I shall proceed with the same spirit I have begun, to the end of my short career. But if neither our former menaces to bereave the French and Spaniards of all their possessions in the West-Indies, nor our deeper laid design, to crush the Dutch at a single stroke, have succeeded to our wish; if every progressive year has seen our losses increase, and our efforts diminish in the same proportion, how mighty, how complete must be the madness that only proposes to end the war with the humiliation of all our enemies!—Are we yet ignorant that war, even in its most successful state, is scarcely less the scourge of the victorious than of the vanquished party? Are we uninformed, that it is most destructive to a commercial country, that depends for its greatness upon a free exportation of its products and manufactures? Do we consider the general failure of every branch of internal industry, with the gradual aberration of the rich streams of external commerce, which formerly enriched us; those aberrations which it is yet uncertain, whether an age of peace and security would completely bring back into their deserted former channels? Will it it not be necessary, before we give a new scope to arrogance and enterprize, to reckon up the vast arrears of the past, and to enquire whether the probable successes of a ten years war, against such formidable opponents, will balance the certain expences of a single year's delay of peace? Are we not already burthened, beyond the possibility of farther endurance; burthened, till even the inventive industry of ministerial ingenuity is forced to pause in its oppressions; lest, by the increase of weight unskilfully applied, the overcharged foundations should give way, and the immense fabric of debts and public credit sink, to rise no more* ? And is it in this situation that the English nation employs itself in forming visionary schemes of grandeur and command, which, were they practicable, might ask at least another seven years bloody war, another hundred millions of expence in the execution? In the mean time, the numerous armies of America surround our few remaining towns, perhaps, flushed with the confidence of victory, and pushed on by the desire of vengeance, lead the scanty remnants of our late victorious bands into captivity; perhaps, in the new ardour of successful enterprize, roll back the tide of war upon our late secure possessions, and assist our enemies to seize all that fortune has hitherto permitted us to retain. At least, even should these ideas be premature, the fatal progress of

our

our evil destiny is continually accelerated, while we waste the precious moments in empty dreams of chimerical exertions; the wounds which we have inflicted upon the Americans, are festering with redoubled anguish; all Europe is preparing to acknowledge their independence, and solicit their alliance; the riches of their commerce, the only resource, I fear, which, even with an immediate peace, would enable us to bear an annual expence of fifteen millions,* are doled out to every competitor; and when some new misfortune shall rouze us from our trance, it may find us reduced so low, as to wish for a return of the present crisis, even at the expence of half our remaining territories.

Let us remember, that it is the characteristic of light and frivolous minds alone to be elated beyond measure with every transient ray of better fortune; to be easily incited to form projects which exceed the compass of their abilities, and to be always ready to throw the blame of past miscarriages upon every thing rather than their own rash and chimerical projects. With such men, the change of a General, or of a Minister, will at any time insure success, and encourage the most extravagant expectations. They cannot believe that heaven, or fortune, will be so unjust

* See Lord Stair's pamphlet.

to their extraordinary merits, as to submit their destiny to the influence of the common causes which controul human affairs; or refuse to work a miracle, whenever a miracle is necessary to extricate them from the effects of their imprudence. Are they citizens, like the Romans, of a state which has risen to importance by severer discipline and stricter manners? They imagine that all the Gods have fixed their residence in the eternal capitol, and will continue to defend the chosen spot, although every virtue which cemented its foundations is withdrawn. But if their country, by a rare coincidence of circumstances, an insular situation, a temperate climate, a system of laws which encourage industry and secure private property, has arrived at commercial and maritime greatness, they mistake these casual blessings for the inherent properties of their soil and climate. They imagine, that they may with impunity engage in every vile and pernicious project, and that their resources will increase in the same proportion that they exhaust and abuse them. Not even the rapid decline of commerce, their own increasing poverty, the miscarriage of their enterprize, the loss of their fairest possessions, their acknowledged incapacity to meet their enemies on the ocean, or their own shores in consequence undefended, and exposed to every invader, can make them abate their arrogance, or lower their pretensions: Nor should

I doubt

I doubt that such a people might gravely claim the empire of the sea, when it had neither commerce, fleet, or seamen left, provided some happy genius should institute a naval procession, or, after the example of the Venetians, proclaim a marriage to be solemnized with the Atlantic.

But it is to be hoped, that the national good sense, when properly applied to the investigation of the subject, will check the desire of military glory, and at length settle in that only measure which can produce any degree of public happiness, a general and substantial peace. Peace is the first and most necessary reform which is required. It is this alone that can restore the almost ruined state of our finances, if that restoration be still possible. A strict and uniform œconomy, applied with unremitting attention, during half a century of peace, might perhaps reduce the public debts within a moderate compass: but what can be expected from our ministers during war, even though they possessed a degree of prudence and disinterestedness which have never yet appeared in man? It is well known that all the schemes of our greatest political œconomists would never have made the public savings amount to half a million; while about three and twenty millions may be calculated to compose the moderate purchase of a single year's continuance of the war. Let my countrymen then seriously reflect upon the accumulation
of

of public debts, such as I believe was never experienced in any other country; upon the intolerable burthens with which every article of convenience, or necessity, is already loaded; and upon forty or fifty additional millions of outstanding debts, which must, in all probability, be directly funded, and new taxes imposed to supply the interest, at least if the declining commerce of the country can support them, before new schemes of enterprize and conquest are adopted. I should then wish to be resolved by some of our ablest calculators, whether the most uninterrupted successes would be likely in any degree to pay the expences they had cost; and whether the fee simple of all the possessions we have lost, excepting the monopoly of the American commerce, which I cannot help supposing out of the question, would indemnify us for a two years continuance of the war. But we have no reason to expect such uninterrupted success from any thing we have yet experienced; and nothing but the most childish presumption, can found a sanguine expectation of better fortune, upon the mere remembrance of past disasters. On the contrary, though we have been repeatedly drawn in, like losing gamesters, to hazard more upon a fresh stake, we have constantly experienced the same catastrophe; nor has there been a single period of six months, which has not degraded us to a worse situation than we were in before, and

augmented

augmented our difficulties both, in refpect to making peace and carrying on the war.—But as to all the paft, however pernicious, however abfurd the conteft may have proved, however defervedly the authors of it may be reprobated as the deliberate enemies of their country, that conteft was lefs abfurd in the beginning, and lefs pernicious in the continuance than it would prove at prefent. It had then a precife and determinate object, however fatal both to humanity and public liberty, the exertion of the legiflative authority of Great Britain over the colonies, or, in more explicit terms, the eftablifhment of unlimited authority, and the reducing them to a ftate of unconditional fervitude. But this object, however execrable, was adapted to pleafe the vanity of a confiderable party in the nation, and few feemed able to difcern the immediate lofs, the ultimate fhame and ruin which might enfue. Although it required no great penetration to forefee that the attempts of this country to extend her authority by force over the colonies, might at fome future period produce their final emancipation, yet fuch was the apparent difproportion of the conteft, that even the cleareft underftandings might doubt concerning the immediate event. But with the prefent experience of our own weaknefs, and the force with which we are to engage, nothing fhort of madnefs can hope for fuccefs in a new attack upon the inde-

I pendence

pendence of America. Indeed, the abfurdity would not be more palpable, were we to revive our ancient pretenfions upon France, and fend over a Mighty armament to annex the territories of his Moft Chriftian Majefty to the crown of England. Were we then to continue an offenfive war, it is plain that it muft now be a war entirely without an object, fince all hopes of fubduing the colonies are at an end; and it muft be a ftruggle of mere difappointed pride and refentment: paffions, which cannot long influence the counfels of nations without the greateft danger, even in their meridian of power and fortune. But as to ourfelves we have too long already been fubject to the influence of thefe blind guides, and wafted too much in rafh and vifionary purfuits. No farther projects, no farther experiments can be tried with fafety, unlefs we choofe to deftroy our remnant of wealth and power, as idly as we have diffipated all the reft. That remnant, if wifely managed, is at leaft fufficient for every purpofe of national happinefs, though not calculated to fatisfy every demand of national vanity. But whatever may be our wifhes or expectations, whether we are difpofed to content ourfelves with the folid enjoyments of fafety and tranquility, or ftill afpire at dangerous preeminence, peace is alike neceffary to the acquifition of either object. Peace alone can deliver us from the enormous burthens with which in-

duftry

duſtry is loaded; or at leaſt prevent the neceſſity of new oppreſſions; peace alone can revive our drooping commerce and agriculture, and enable us, by wiſe and ſalutary laws, and internal efforts at improvement, to increaſe our population and manufactures. Peace would enable us to turn our attention at leiſure, to the immenſe territories we poſſeſs in India; a territory ſo vaſt, ſo fertile, ſo well peopled, that it might compenſate many of our loſſes, could we be convinced of the neceſſity of regulating it by wholeſome laws, adapted to the genius of the inhabitants, inſtead of making it the theatre where European plunderers contend for pillage. Peace would make us more reſpected in all the dependencies which we yet retain, and probably eradicate the ſeeds of future civil wars, if we do not think it below our dignity to be taught wiſdom by our paſt experience, or unworthy our greatneſs to redreſs the juſt complaints we have occaſioned by our former oppreſſions.

I ſhall now proceed to ſtate thoſe articles of the treaty of alliance between France and America, ſigned at Paris, February 6, 1778, which relate to the preſent ſubject, and prove the improbability of the colonies liſtening to any ſeparate terms of peace, before the acknowledgment of their independence. The ſecond article of that treaty expreſsly ſtates, that " The eſſential and direct end " of the preſent defenſive alliance is, to maintain " effectually

"effectually the liberty, sovereignty and inde-
"pendence, absolute and unlimited, of the said
"United States, as well in matters of government
"as of commerce." The 8th article is "Neither
"of the two parties shall conclude either truce or
"peace with Great Britain without the formal
"consent of the other first obtained; and they
"mutually engage not to lay down their arms,
"until the independence of the United States,
"shall have been formally or tacitly assured by
"the treaty or treaties that shall terminate the
"war." This I should think is sufficient to prove how visionary and unfounded were the opinions which lately prevailed with many of my countrymen, that the Americans would obey the first invitation of this country to desert the French, and even league with us against them. Nothing but the same ignorance and inattention which have guided every other part of our conduct could possibly have produced such a judgment.

But a more specious and important consequence may be deduced from the articles I have quoted: that even should the English allow the independence of the Colonies in the most unequivocal manner, they are so involved with France, that they would not have it in their power to suspend hostilities without the permission of their allies. This interpretation is certainly not unauthorized, and is a sufficient comment upon the wisdom of those, thofe, who, in fpite of the moſt authentic information, fuffered the Americans to enter into fuch clofe connections with our enemies, at a time when it is probable a little moderation and vigilance on our part would have prevented them. But when we confider the fenfe of the fecond article, which explains and limits the nature of the alliance, we fhall find that it exprefsly declares it to be defenfive for the purpofe of maintaining the fovereignty and independence of the United States. Again, the 8th article confirms this interpretation by limiting the duration of the war to the acknowledgment of the independence of America. The obvious and literal fenfe of this treaty therefore is to ratify a defenfive union between France and America, for the purpofe of eſtabliſhing the independence of the latter; and this end once obtained, leaves both the contracting parties at liberty. Nor can much doubt be entertained that the Americans themfelves will confider it in this light, and not think it neceffary to carry on a war for the intereſt of their allies, againſt a nation with whom they have fo many natural connections; and in whofe favour we may rationally fuppofe fo many ancient prejudices will arife, the inſtant all ideas of farther perfecution are removed. It is the intereſt of the contracting parties, which is alone the guardian and interpreter of treaties between independent ſtates; and this intereſt will evidently

evidently run as much in favour of England, when England difcovers unequivocal inclinations for peace, as it did before, againſt her. It was the intereſt of France to feparate fo large a portion of territory from Great-Britain, whom ſhe juſtly confiders as her moſt formidable enemy; it was equally her intereſt to throw down all barriers to the American commerce, which opened fuch unbounded views to the ingenuity of her manufacturers, and fuch ample refources to the embarraſſments of her finances. Nor was it lefs the intereſt of the Americans to accept the overtures and alliance of every power which was hoſtile to this country, and offered to fupport their independence againſt its attacks. An alliance founded upon thefe principles, will neceſſarily remain firm and indiſſoluble, fo long as the common intereſts of the contracting parties coalefce: but let either of them completely acquire the objects of its wiſhes, and ample fcope is given to all the motives of envy, jealoufy, and diſtruſt, to exert their power, and gradually corrode the bands of union.

Thus, it appears evident, in whatever light we confider the fubject, that acknowledging the independence of America, is a neceſſary preliminary of peace: for it will either fo completely fatisfy the intereſt and ambition of all our enemies, that no material oppoſition will be made to its ratification;

cation; or should it fail to have that effect, will render the Americans so luke-warm and indifferent to the common cause, that we may naturally promise ourselves happier fortune against our remaining enemies.

Some gentlemen indeed seem to imagine, that it is not necessary to make such sacrifices, and that a reconciliation may be effected with America, on terms similar to what we have granted the Irish. But till they shall take the trouble of explaining the reasons of this opinion, I cannot help thinking that it is more calculated to flatter the remains of national pride, than founded upon any real knowledge of the subject.

It is no secret that a commission has been sent over from the American congress to five commissioners in Europe to treat of peace, whenever Great-Britain shall be inclined to accede to those terms which are essential to its conclusion: It is also certain that several of the American agents, amongst whom Dr. Franklin may be numbered, have, both in their conversation and letters expressed the most sincere desire of terminating the present waste of human blood, by a speedy reconciliation with this country; nor do I doubt that there is still sufficient affection remaining in the minds of many of the Americans, to make them desire every degree of prosperity to this country, which is consistent with the freedom,

interest

interest, and honour of their own. It is also equally certain, that not one of these commissioners, amongst whom are included Dr. Franklin, Mr. Adams, and Mr. Laurens, have ever given the present ministry the least hope that any part of America would relinquish its independence, for any terms or advantages proposed by Great-Britain; on the contrary, I have every reason to believe, that this has been the uniform language of all the American agents who have been consulted upon the subject: " Great-Britain by her
" pride, her insolence, her unjust attempts to re-
" duce the colonies to servitude, has compelled
" them to resist by arms the intended invasion of
" their rights. In the prosecution of this justifi-
" able resistance, they have declared themselves
" independent; because, neither duty, compact,
" nor allegiance, can subsist between the oppres-
" sor and the oppressed; between the nation that
" aims a mortal stroke at the existence of ano-
" ther, and the people that takes up defensive
" arms to vindicate itself from slavery and de-
" struction. But Providence has uniformly blast-
" ed the ambitious designs of England, and fa-
" voured the struggles of the Thirteen States, that
" through such difficulties, through so many va-
" rious fortunes, through such a storm of blood
" and death, have persevered in the generous
" design of maintaining the rights of nature and

the

" the common cause of the human species. If
" Great-Britain, unenlightened by all the past, un-
" taught by her own calamities, still persists in her
" former arrogance, and dreams of binding the
" hitherto unconquerable minds of the Americans,
" let her collect all her remaining forces, and ga-
" ther auxiliary troops of mercenaries from all
" the tyrants that deal in human blood, to make
" a last decisive trial of her fortune. She has
" already abridged all other rights, and severed
" every other tie, by appealing to the sword; and
" the sword is now the only charter of dominion,
" by which she must hope to rule over American
" subjects. Does she imagine that the ghastly
" wounds of a seven years civil war are to be
" closed in an instant by the charm of a fallacious
" lenity? Or that the Americans can so soon for-
" get the injuries they have received, their pro-
" perty wasted, their towns destroyed, their coun-
" try desolated, and every degree of hostile in-
" sult and cruelty offered to their families and
" themselves? Are these the potent arguments
" which are to induce them to resign the price
" of all their victories, and trust themselves again
" to the compassion of a British government, at
" the expence of all that is manly, just, or noble,
" either in nations or individuals? Is it for
" these benefits, so feelingly enforced, that they
" are to desert allies that have supported

K   them

" them in the hour of danger, cherished the ris-
" ing hopes of their infant states, and dared the
" vengeance and the shock of the proudest, if
" not the most powerful nation in the universe?
" Or does the same delusion which made the En-
" glish promise themselves so easy a conquest in
" the beginning, make them now imagine that
" the Americans are to be subdued by policy,
" after having proved themselves unconquerable
" by arms? Why else do they think of proposing
" terms which they must know would be rejected
" with scorn by every people that is not delivered
" up to infatuation? Shall the Americans brand
" themselves with every epithet of perfidy and
" falsehood, violate the unblemished honour of
" their new republicks, and deprive themselves of
" the future favour and assistance of all Europe,
" that must be witness of their shameful ingrati-
" tude, only that they may deliver themselves up
" to the very people that has been so long armed
" for their destruction.—They are not so igno-
" rant of the feelings of established governments
" towards those that are denominated rebels, or
" what they must themselves expect even from the
" moment of their accepting so sinister a league.
" As to the pretended concessions which are some-
" times made to rebellious subjects, they are at
" best but authorized frauds, to disarm the intended
" victims of future cruelty and revenge. Is there
" in

" in all the wide extent of hiftory, that baneful
" catalogue of human crimes and miferies, a
" fingle inftance of thefe involuntary conceffions
" which has not been revoked, without regard
" to faith or humanity, the very moment when it
" might be attempted with impunity? And what
" is there in the nature of the Britifh govern-
" ment, that fhould produce an exception in its
" favour? We are not ignorant of the mutability
" and inconfiftency of its counfels; thofe coun-
" fels which fometimes menace the fecurity and
" independence of all the furrounding nations,
' fometimes folicit peace with the holy fervour of
" primitive Chriftianity. If the Englifh themfelves
" repofe an implicit faith in her new adminiftra-
" tion, it is not fo with the Americans, it is not
" fo with the reft of mankind. We know that
" the fame breath which has blown up the bubble,
" that now dances upon the atmofphere of nati-
" onal conceit, may diffipate its unfubftantial fa-
" bric, and breathe again thofe peftilential vapours
" which lately threatened the deftruction of half
" mankind. As to the Englifh themfelves, if they
" have voluntarily joined in this profcription of
" the Americans, what faith, what confidence is
" to be given to a barbarous unfeeling nation,
" that only fufpends its cruelties from an inability
" to purfue them?—If, on the contrary, as fome
" pretend, they have been reluctantly compelled

K 2   to

"to fanctify outrages which they difapprove, on
"what pretence do they attempt to modify the
"rights of others, who are incapable of defending
"their own. Let them therefore underſtand, that
"whether their characteriſtic be cruelty or weakneſs,
"we will neither confide in the one, nor ſhare in the
"miſchievous conſequences of the other. We
"will remain fixed to that ſpot where fortune and
"Providence have eſtabliſhed the foundations of
"our riſing empire, by the agency of our own
"fortitude and virtue. If England thinks that
"ſhe can puſh us from the ſolid baſis on which
"we now ſtand firm, let her approach with all
"her remaining forces, and make the dangerous
"experiment. If, on the contrary, ſhe has had ſuf-
"ficient experience of her own weakneſs, and wiſhes
"to give the world and herſelf ſome interval of
"repoſe, let her, as a preliminary, defiſt from all
"the ſchemes of wild and fruitleſs ambition. Let
"her equally lay aſide the projects of fraud and
"violence; nor attempt, by the contemptible
"arts of crooked policy, to deceive thoſe whom
"ſhe is unable to conquer. Let her meet the
"Americans with ſincerity and magnanimity; let
"her make all the atonement which is within
"her power to thoſe ſhe has injured, by defiſting
"from new attempts to injure. As to our inde-
"pendence, in the ampleſt ſenſe that can be given
"to the term, we do not aſk it of England or her
                                         miniſters

" minifters, becaufe it is not theirs to give; we
" already hold it from Heaven and the points of
" our fwords; and upon thefe alone fhall we de-
" pend for its prefervation. Yet if fhe fairly and
" honourably treat with us upon thefe terms, we
" fhall acknowledge it as a proof of her fincerity,
" and accept it as a pledge of offered peace. By
" thefe means, the memory of paft injuries may
" be gradually obliterated, and fhe may yet find
" in a participation of our commerce, the fureft
" prop of her declining opulence, and in our
" returning affection and future alliance, no con-
" temptible fupport of her remaining empire.
" But let her at length underftand the real limits
" of her power, and defift from the attempt
" to unite and reconcile contradictions. The
" two alternatives are indeed before her,
" and fhe may take her choice; a firm and
" profitable peace, accompanied with the inde-
" pendence of the colonies, or a war of hatred,
" revenge, and fury to reduce the Americans to
" fervitude, or perifh in the attempt. More than
" this, neither fortune, nor Heaven allows; nor
" her own ungovernable madnefs, which has com-
" pelled the Americans to feize that independence
" which fhe now in vain endeavours to withold,
" and compleated the difmemberment of the em-
" pire."

This,

This, or nearly this, I have reason to believe, has been the language of the American agents, whenever they have been consulted: should I be mistaken, or endeavour to mislead, it will be no difficult matter to convict me of ignorance or falsehood. In the mean time, I cannot help supposing this representation to be a just one, and drawing some conclusions from it, which merit all the attention of the public.

It must appear evident, that no conclusion whatever can be admitted from the situation of the Irish to that of the Americans, excepting that a weak and oppressive government will produce similar effects in every part of its dominions. The Irish have obtained every thing they demanded: they asked for a free trade; that free trade has been granted them; they disclaimed the authority of the British parliament; that point too has been given up; and they now declare themselves, as they have every reason to be, contented with the concessions of the government. They have never voted themselves independent, never entered into foreign alliances, never seen their country ravaged, or themselves proscribed, under the pretence of restoring constitutional liberty and happiness. There can be little doubt that the half of these concessions offered to the Americans, when they petitioned in the year 1775, would have preserved their union with this country inviolate, and prevented

vented all the mischiefs which have since ensued. But that period is irretrievably past, and never can return. The colonies are now in actual possession of independence; they have constituted internal governments, which may perhaps leave them little to regret in their loss of the British constitution; they have formed alliances with other nations, upon the solemn compact of never again submitting to a dependence, either upon this country or crown; they have repeatedly foiled the attempts of Great Britain to reduce them to her dependence, and refused to treat upon any other footing than that of independent nations. What is there in all this, similar to the present, or past state of Ireland; and what can be meant by the proposal of offering to the Americans the same terms we have granted to the Irish, unless a pretext for involving this country in all the miseries of a new war, to support propositions which we are sure will be rejected with contempt?—Will these terms be offered to the Congress?—But the Congress have no more power or right to accept them, than the British parliament would have to abdicate the independence of this country, and make it an appendage to France or Spain —Nay less.—For a British parliament we all know is omnipotent; an attribute which I believe has never yet been claimed by Congress, who are only the deputies of the several states, to transact whatever business

relates

relates to the common interests of the confederacy. Beside, we have some reason to guess at their sentiments upon this subject, by their treatment of the British Commissioners in the year 1778.— Shall we then offer these gracious terms to each of the several states that compose the American confederacy? But I have yet heard of no overtures from any of the provincial governments, which should make us hope that they would be accepted; and we know it to be a fundamental article of the American union, that any state, which shall presume to treat of a separate peace, shall be accounted a deserter of the common cause, and a public enemy. No way therefore would remain, as we can neither expect the Congress, or any of the provincial governments, to treat with us upon these terms, but to have the gracious proposals of a repentant government printed and dispersed over the country, for the benefit of individuals. And as the Americans have already had some experience of our methods of protecting them, I leave every one to conjecture the probable success of such a measure; more especially if we add to it the late vote of the House of Commons against carrying on an offensive war in America. In the mean time I should fear, that these inconveniences might result from such a step. The Congress would not fail to pass the most indignant votes upon the occasion; they, and all the friends of

the

the eſtabliſhed governments, would paint this conduct of the Engliſh nation in the blackeſt colours of perfidy and deceit. They would repreſent us as a nation devoid of honeſty and ſincerity; ſo determinately inimical to the liberties of America, that we never, even when we aſſumed the moſt pacific appearances, could lay aſide the idea of enſlaving the colonies; that, as our hoſtilities were replete with every ſpecies of cruelty, ſo were our negociations with treachery and falſehood. What are theſe " pretended
" offers, would they add, but a repetition of the
" ſame inſidious arts, which they have ſo often
" ineffectually tried already? They know your
" prudence, and your valour, when united; they
" know that you are neither to be ſubdued by
" force, nor circumvented by negociation, and
" therefore they again have recourſe to their
" wonted arts, and attempt to diſſolve that union
" which renders you ſo formidable. It is im-
" poſſible for that haughty nation to conſider you
" in any other light than that of ſlaves, eman-
" cipated for a moment, but deſtined ſooner or
" later to return to her domination. Even when
" all the reſt of Europe ſhall have admitted your
" independence, and ſolicited your alliance, you
" will be honoured with no other title than that
" of rebels by Great-Britain. The hatred that
" ſhe nouriſhes againſt you, for your emancipa-

L " tion

" tion, is as unchangeable and eternal as her
" purpose of reducing you again to her do-
" minion, and making you pay the accumulated
" punishment of your too succesful resistance.
" This is the spirit which alike animates her wars,
" and dictates her proposals of peace. In the
" one, she has ever been a cruel and vindictive
" enemy; in the other, she is a false, insidious
" friend. Even now, amidst all her professions
" of returning amity, she cannot hide the venom
" which is rankling in her heart, or conceal the
" intolerable arrogance which has so long guided
" all her counsels.—Does she offer to treat about
" a peace so necessary to her own affairs?—It is
" in such a manner, as proves, that she still con-
" siders herself as your rightful sovereign, and you
" as revolted subjects, on whom she confers a
" favour, in remitting some part of your merited
" punishment. Though baffled so often, and
" disgraced, she still treats with you as a superior;
" and thinks the honour of her alliance cheaply
" purchased by you, at the expence of national
" honour and independence. Yes, that very in-
" dependence which you possess as absolutely as
" any people in the universe, she pretends to mo-
" dify, and graciously contenting herself with
" bereaving you of more than half your rights,
" is willing that you should hold the rest by the
" charter of her concession. But it is impossible

that

" that you should be deceived by such contemp-
" tible arts as these; or accept the olive as a pledge
" of peace, whose leaves are incapable of con-
" cealing the serpent which entwines its branches.
" Her offers are too openly insidious, and the
" malignity of her intentions breaks forth too
" glaringly, through the veil of dissembled friend-
" ship, with which she endeavours to conceal it.
" She sees the impossibility of conquering you in
" the field, and therefore has recourse to nego-
" ciations, which she hopes may win their way
" where arms would fail. She wishes to make
" you lose the confidence of your allies, and the
" esteem of Europe; thus will you be the more
" exposed to her future machinations. She
" wishes to scatter feuds, disunion and distrust
" amongst the several states that compose the
" American confederacy, and to arm them one
" against the other, that the whole may be more
" easily oppressed and enslaved. This is the
" reason why she refuses to treat with those
" whom you have appointed to be the arbiters of
" peace and war. She knows too well their vigi-
" lance, their prudence, their inflexibility; she
" fears to meet the guardians of your liberty in
" council, as much as to encounter your armies
" in the field; she therefore endeavours to ensnare
" the ignorance and credulity of individuals, and
" by scattering secret discontents and jealousies,

" to open a way for her usurpations. But go-
" vernments that are founded upon principles of
" justice, and who claim no power but what is
" given them by common suffrage, are unac-
" quainted with the fears and low suspicions which
" never fail to accompany tyranny. We there-
" fore submit her proposals to you, conscious
" that there is but one light in which every friend
" to American liberty can consider them. Nor
" do we fear, that those who have toiled so
" nobly through such a contest, to establish the
" foundations of the only free governments in the
" universe, will tamely yield, without an equiva-
" lent, the reward of all their labours."

Should any one be disposed to treat me as the advocate of American independence for expatiating upon these topics; without either confessing or denying the charge, I must observe, that it is entirely foreign to the purpose. No one can doubt that the Congress will refuse our overtures for the future dependence of America, should such overtures be made. Nor will they be contented with a simple refusal; it is equally certain, that they will employ their whole address to represent these overtures, in the blackest colours, to the body of the people. Whether they are actuated by a noble ambition of raising the glory of their country, or by the low desire of preserving their own authority alone, this will equally be their
conduct.

conduct. Even the advocates for propofing to the Americans terms fimilar to thofe we have granted the Irifh, are of this opinion; fince they affert, that neither the agents of the French, nor of the Congrefs, will be able to prevent the reconciliation which they imagine muſt be the confequence of fuch liberal conceffions. No one therefore can accufe me of fingularity for entertaining an opinion, which is even admitted by thofe who differ widely from me as to the reſt; and the reflections which I have attributed to the Congrefs, are fuch as muft prefent themfelves even to the moft fuperficial underſtandings.

Placed as I am, at an awful diſtance from the profound myſteries of government, I cannot pretend to decypher accurately the intentions of our rulers. Many circumſtances may make it inexpedient that the mazes of ſtate-policy fhould be expofed to vulgar eyes; and therefore we ought to wait with a becoming patience, for the fuccefs of thofe negociations which are now carrying on. But it is impoffible for any man who has been an anxious witnefs of the public calamities, during the prefent ill-omened conteſt, not to form conjectures about the future. Thefe conjectures it is the diſtinguifhed privilege of every Engliſhman to dare to offer to the public; the meaneſt citizen enjoys this right in common with the proudeſt; and the experience of fome paſt years does not tend

tend to prove, that either virtue or ability is engrossed by those who possess the highest stations.

I shall therefore observe, that the terms now offered to the Americans, either contain an acknowledgment of their independence, or proposals for some limited dependence on this country. In the first case, there is little reason to doubt, that they will be attended with the desired success: and a peace will be no longer delayed than till the different claims of the contending parties can be adjusted. On the second supposition, I will venture to predict, that all proposals for the dependence of America on Great-Britain, however modified, will be rejected with scorn by the Congress, and all the ruling powers in that country. I have sufficiently stated my reasons for this assertion; but it is a speculation of the most interesting nature to enquire, what will be the conduct of our ministers in case of such a refusal.

Some persons may possess that fervour of imagination, which may lead them to think, that the revolution of power in this country will produce a similar one on the other side of the Atlantic. They doubtless dream, that when the British offers shall be dispersed over the country, the people will either compel their rulers to accept them, or take up arms to depose both Magistrates and Congress; that all America will forget both republicanism and independence, and unite to celebrate the

praises

praises of a patriot administration, in a transport of gratitude and loyalty. As to myself, whatever joy it would give me to see the inhabitants of Boston and Philadelphia approaching the throne with loyal and constitutional addresses, I cannot help fearing, that we are far removed from such an auspicious æra. We know that the attachment of mankind, either to national manners or forms of government, bears no proportion to the comparative excellence of the objects; if indeed it be possible to establish a criterion to judge of things which are reducible to no common principles, and which vary with every gust of national prejudice or opinion. All the representations of European elegance or enjoyment, would no more tempt a Kamtschatkan from his cave, or an Iroquois from his forest, than the love of savage liberty and independence would induce an English nobleman to throw aside the trappings of his exalted station, and take refuge in eternal snows, or pathless deserts. How often do we see the opinions that in one country are treated as the excess of wickedness and impiety, consecrated by altars, priests, and temples, amidst their neighbours; while the reverence for a particular name or family, which is considered as loyalty and honour on one side of a river or mountain, shall be reprobated as treason and rebellion on the other!—Whatever reverence, therefore,

therefore, we may feel for the English constitution, whatever blessings we may imagine it capable of imparting, it is impossible to deny, that the Americans may entertain very different ideas upon the subject. The splendour of a court, the advantages of an hereditary monarchy, the sacred name of King itself may be in some minds so strongly associated with the ideas of unlimited power, and the purpose of enslaving mankind, that they may excite no favourable impressions. Whether from reason, obstinacy, or error, we know that these are the sentiments of the Americans; at least a large, if not the largest part of this nation has been accustomed to represent them in this light. But if the natural bent of their dispositions has long inclined them to independence and republicanism, it will be difficult to assign a reason why they should entertain more moderate ideas at present.

But should they persist in these ideas, should they reject the offered terms with the contempt which I am persuaded they will feel for every proposal of dependence, what conduct is this country to observe?—Are we to depart, at length, from all our lofty pretensions, and grant the long-contested boon; are all the fine-spun schemes of political connection to be dissolved; all hopes of returning allegiance to be sacrificed; are fifty thousand lives, and an hundred millions

of

of treafure to be wafted in vain, and only to cement the foundation of thirteen republican ftates: or will our minifters, animated by a noble defpair, pafs all the bounds which they had before prefcribed, and heedlefs alike of their own profeffions and the infamy which muft attend fuch grofs inconfiftency, openly engage themfelves in a new war to fubdue the Colonies?

This enquiry is of fo much importance, that the illuftrious characters who compofe the prefent adminiftration will certainly give the people complete fatisfaction upon the fubject. They know how much we have already fuffered, how repeatedly the public confidence has been abufed already by former minifters; they have long and feelingly arraigned the bafe duplicity and falfehood which ufed to prevail in our councils; and it is to refcue us from evils like thefe, not from avarice or ambition, or the felfifh defire of advancing themfelves upon the ruin of others that they have accepted the reins of government; every motive of honour, fhame, confiftency muft incline them to a nobler conduct; nor will they deceive our wifhes, or adopt the execrable arts to which we owe fo many miferies.

Should they therefore be convinced that the dignity of the crown, the fpirit of the conftitution, the unity of the empire, require new wars, new facrifices, and the impofition of heavier burthens, they will at least treat the public with sincerity, and acquaint it with the important change in their sentiments. This change may indeed happen, because there is the greatest difference between a ministry and an opposition, and many sources of information and motives of conduct must occur to the one which are totally denied the other. But they will lay before us the reasons which they now find to expect success, in schemes which they have so often declared impracticable; they will state the remaining resources of the nation that inspire them with these hopes, the intended expence and probable duration of the war. They will not inveigle us from year to year with false estimates and fallacious hopes; nor will they delude the unwary innocence of the country gentlemen with promises of lowering their taxes from the confiscations and forfeitures of America. Should it be necessary to send over new armies with better auspices, they will not do it under the mean pretence of defending ports, or garrisoning towns. They will also, I hope, think it necessary to assign the limits of their own exertions, and the period at which we may expect some respite, whatever be the fortunes of the war. Wherever these limits may be fixed, whether at public bankruptcy, a seizure of all private property for the use of government, or the general depopulation of the land, it will be some alleviation of our distresses, to look forward to a certain termination; and it will enable those who

want

want faith or loyalty to wait the last extremity, to seek over the habitable globe some asylum from the blessings of the English constitution.

In the mean time I shall endeavour to state those reasons which induce me to believe that our present administration have either already acceded to the independence of America, or mean to do it, if that condition should be insisted upon as a preliminary of peace. Those gentlemen while they were out of power have been accustomed to make the American war the subject of their severest and most popular invectives. According to them, the design to subdue the colonies was equally unjust, absurd, and ruinous. All the forces of the British empire were inadequate to such an attempt, and public bankruptcy must be the necessary consequence of persisting in the enterprize. With what energy, with what eloquence have they descanted upon our declining commerce, our involved finances, the distresses of our country gentlemen, the miseries of the poor, and all the complicated calamities which this unnatural quarrel has produced. How often and how feelingly have they adjured the late administration to stop the ravages of war, to restore peace to an exhausted nation, and to offer the Americans such terms as they were likely to accept. With these sentiments so often, and so solemnly expressed, they have entered upon the management of public affairs,

affairs, in order to rescue their country from its difficulties by a speedy peace. But it is impossible they could mistake the terms upon which alone it was attainable. They were not ignorant of the treaties the Americans had entered into with France, of the answers of the Congress to former propositions, of the representations of the American agents; every thing concurred to enforce the necessity of independence, as a preliminary or condition of peace. Unless therefore they intended giving up this article, their invectives and their professions must have been alike empty and insincere. For what was the crime of the last administration, at least after the commencement of the war, and the treaty of alliance, but refusing to grant the independence of America, and prosecuting the war to make her forego that claim? That administration never refused to treat on terms short of independence, nor did the Americans ever make any conciliatory proposals to that purpose since the year 1776. But those ministers had repeatedly declared, that they never would acknowledge the independence of America, or desist from war till the colonies had given up the claim; and it was to save us from the inevitable ruin which must have attended so rash and absurd a resolution, that the rising spirit of the nation has produced the present happy change. But this change has not been effected merely that the people might be amused with a vain shadow of negociation; this was a task for which our late ministers were as well qualified as their successors. Nor was it from the hope that the Americans would recede from their haughty declarations of independence, in favour of a new administration; such a system might amuse the politicians of a coffeehouse, or the editor of a newspaper, but was too ridiculous and unfounded to be adopted by men of sense, who possessed the genuine sources of information. Least of all was it, merely that the conduct of the war might be shuffled from one hand to another: it is the war itself, and not the management of it, that the late opposition have so successfully arraigned; nor have they ever succeeded so well in proving the incapacity of the late ministers for carrying it on, as in demonstrating that the proposed end itself was chimerical, unjust, and unattainable. But it was to stop the ravages of that pernicious war; to vindicate our declining commerce and agriculture from new and more intolerable burthens; to restore plenty to their country, and peace to Europe, that men of milder principles, the patrons of public liberty, and the genuine friends of the people, have been elevated to the honours they now enjoy.

Hence it seems to follow, that every friend of the present administration should strenuously vindicate them from the suspicion of meditating any coercive war against America. Such a charge must either include the excess of folly or duplicity—folly, if they alone were ignorant of facts which every man of common abilities or information clearly understood; and duplicity, if all their declamations in favour of peace meaned nothing more than to acquire the management of the war. But that degree of ignorance was absolutely impossible: nothing therefore remains but to accuse them of the grossest insincerity. For if, in the present situation of England, the public interest required that we should carry on a war to reduce our colonies to some modified degree of dependence, what must we think of men who have uniformly opposed the very measures they are compelled to adopt at last? We know too well the uncertain nature of war; that an opportunity once lost is frequently never to be regained; and the influence which the opinion of vigour and perseverance exercises over the minds of men, so great and universal, that mankind are much oftner conquered by their own fears than by the prowess of their enemies. The last ministry had some title to both these qualities; they lavished the blood and treasures of the nation as profusely as if centuries of duration were comprized in the present moment, and as if America once nominally subdued would set us free from any future struggle; nor did they ever pretend to humanity or remorse;

they

they plainly declared, with a moſt laudable ſincerity, that if they could not conquer America, they wiſhed to render it an uninhabited deſert, a ſmoaking pile of ruins. This was plain and manly; it was alſo conſiſtent with a certain ſet of principles, which has generally had the ſanction of divines, and, for the curſe of human nature, has always been the favourite creed of princes and ſtateſmen. But what would have been the conduct of their antagoniſts upon the ſuppoſition I am now examining? Equally convinced of the fatal neceſſity of theſe meaſures, they muſt have uſed their whole addreſs and influence to render them abortive, when their ſucceſs would have been attended with leſs loſs and blood-ſhed than it would be at preſent; or elſe, againſt their own conviction, they muſt become the miniſters of cruelty and injuſtice, and deſolate the world merely that they may preſerve their places. The celebrated vote of the Houſe of Commons againſt proſecuting an offenſive war with America, was certainly the work of the late minority; and this vote was a plain confeſſion to all the world of our weakneſs and inability to purſue the war. That vote, with more than magic force, arreſted all our military operations, diſarmed our veteran bands, and added confidence and intrepidity to their enemies. That vote was a compleat abdication of all our boaſted ſovereignty over America, and

and gave additional stability both to the Provincial governments and the authority of the Congress. For is it possible that after such a declaration we could invite a single American to join our banners, or expose ourselves to his derision, by promising our protection? To me indeed, and to every man that is not possessed with the chimerical rage of making conquests, that vote appeared the only mark of public sanity which we have shewn for many years. Considered as the pledge and harbinger of approaching peace, it seemed wisely calculated to abate the animosity of the colonies, and merited all our gratitude and approbation; but if it was nothing more than a public leger-de main to juggle the cards out of hand into another, it certainly was the grossest instance of public absurdity that ever was exhibited. Nor would it solve the objection to suppose, that no offensive war was to be waged with the Americans, but only with the French, till they gave up the treaty of alliance and the independence of the colonies. If the French demand immoderate terms of peace, we shall be compelled to carry on a war, not against the independence of America, but for our defence. But it will be necessary to prove this in a satisfactory manner, both to this nation and to Europe at large, by exposing the terms that had been offered by us, and refused by them, otherwise it must appear the vilest political quibble that

ever

ever disgraced a nation; and only intended to lull one enemy asleep, till we had dispatched the rest, and could return with additional force for his destruction. Such conduct I am afraid, instead of serving, would only prejudice our cause in the eyes of all mankind, by adding the imputation of treachery to that of violence; and would so totally alienate the Americans, by raising unconquerable suspicions of our sincerity, as would render all reconciliation impossible.

Nothing therefore remains but to suppose, that as our ministers are men of sense, and pledged to the people by every motive that can act on generous minds, they really mean to pursue that conduct which honour and public utility equally require; and to give us that peace, which it is certainly in their power to bestow, and which our difficulties and distresses so loudly demand. This is certainly the wish of the founder, and I believe at present of the most numerous part of the nation; and the experience of every hour will add new converts to the opinion. Whatever may be the frantic exultations or chimerical projects of a few, the wiser individuals of every party, think that we have made a sufficient trial of fortune, and that the present strength of our enemies is so overproportioned to our own, that it is a sufficient glory to have been so well able to act upon the defensive. They see that the project of destroying the navies of France, Spain and Holland, is as chimerical as it is unjuft; and that were it more practicable than it is, the reft of Europe is too intent upon its own commercial interefts, to fuffer the balance of naval power to be entirely deftroyed, and fo great an acceffion of ftrength thrown into hands that have not always ufed it with the greateft moderation. As to America, all parties are now agreed, excepting a few hot-headed zealots, that fhe has nothing to fear from the attacks of England; and that no future connection can fubfift between the two countries, but the voluntary ties of friendfhip and mutual intereft.

In this fituation, every thing concurs to make the people defirous of accepting peace, and to induce the miniftry to grant it. Every order of men will rejoice to fee a termination of public difficulties and impofitions excepting the few who might have promoted a vile, partial intereft, by the continuation of the war. Whatever may be the murmurs of that fet of men, they will foon fubfide, extinguifhed by the voice of a grateful nation, that will fooner or later learn, by its own comparative feelings, the difference between a full and fafe enjoyment of the fruits of its induftry, a circumftance fo neceffary to all, and the empty triumphs of fuch a war as we now carry on always balanced by contrary fortune, and attended by increafing poverty and diftrefs. Thefe reflexions

flexions appear to me so solid and unanswerable, and at the same time so important to this country in the present moment, that I could not resist the impulse of laying them before the public; whatever personal danger or inconvenience may attend the publication of unpalatable truths, so little disguised by artifice or flattery, that they may disgust even those who cannot dispute their authority.

It may be asked, why I alone have thus stood forth, and pretended to instruct a nation. Many will tax me with folly and presumption; many will arraign me as the friend of America, and enemy to the glory of my country; some may perhaps accuse me of secret interest, or disguised ambition. As to any of these charges, I should consider them with indifference and contempt, did not the nature of my subject itself prevent me from passing them over in silence. I shall therefore observe, that what I have here advanced, is little calculated to gain me either patronage or popularity; none but the real, disinterested friends of their country, will either excuse the doctrines, or the boldness with which they are enforced; and the only character I can ever expect to gain by means like these, is, that of a turbulent, discontented man, incapable of leaguing with any party, and dangerous to all. As to the presumption which I have used, it is no greater than becomes a man, than, I think, becomes an Englishman; every one is equally interested in the welfare of that society of which he is a member; the meanest can but lose his all in common with the greatest; nor are the trappings of state and gewgaws of a crown of more importance to the monarch, than his cottage and humble fare to a peasant: neither nature, reason, or justice, has given to a few individuals the right of judging for all the rest.

But as to the heavier charge of favouring the liberties of America, far from attempting an apology, I shall both confess and glory in the accusation. England is indeed my country; there was a time when I gloried in the name; and I will presume to say, that few have shewn themselves more completely English, either in their principles or conduct, than myself. But I have never been able to cherish an exclusive partiality for any country at the expence of justice and humanity; and were I capable of doing it, the result of all my experience tends to convince me, that the real interest of no society ever was, or will be promoted by systems which contradict the plainest principles of morality. The widest range of empire, the most uninterrupted successes which have attended the guilty projects of ambition, have never produced any other effect, than that

of

of hurrying nations so much the more rapidly to their decline.

And much would it conduce both to the security and happiness of mankind, were this great truth more clearly understood, or more universally adopted as the principle of action. We might then expect to see honest ends pursued by honourable means; and a care of the essential interests of the people substituted to the paltry intrigues and machinations which have so long been the disgrace of courts and statesmen. Those who claimed superior privileges, or engrossed the powers and distinctions of society, would think it necessary to deserve them by other arts than a contemptible luxury, an habitual practice of low dissimulation, or a blind acquiescence in those pernicious schemes which alike sap the foundations of liberty and public happiness. In peace, we should see them intent on repairing the ravages of war, improving every means of national defence, regulating the morals, and adding to the convenience of the people. Their care and wisdom would correct every abuse, before it increased to a dangerous magnitude; nor would the art of legislation remain the greatest reproach to the human understanding, and the least improved by the progress of reason and philosophy. The laws, whose clearness and intelligibility are so essential to the happiness of the people, would be adapted to
common

common ufe and underſtandings; not by reducing them to one general principle of promiſcuous deſpotiſm, an improvement which many of their profeſſors are ſo deſirous of introducing, but by difentangling them from the cuſtoms and perplexity of barbarous ages, from the doubtful force of contrary deciſions, and all the unmeaning rubbiſh in which they are now involved. Commerce and agriculture would flouriſh, not by the regulations of boards of trade, or the thouſand abſurd and contradictory proviſions which difgrace our ſtatutes, and deter the honeſt mechanic from the exertion of his ingenuity, but by ſecuring to every man the produce of his labours, freeing induſtry from unneceſſary reſtraints, and bounding the incroachments of that all-devouring monſter the exciſe. Were it neceſſary to engage in wars, thoſe wars would be ſo clearly juſt and unavoidable, that there could be no difpute about the expedience of ſupporting them: a wife œconomy would manage thoſe reſources which are drawn from the labours of the people, nor would the public confidence itſelf be made a reaſon for its abuſe, or the public patience an apology for the profuſion of a government.

Theſe indeed are viſionary ſchemes, ſufficient to interrupt the gravity of a miniſter, ſhould he condeſcend to read them, or move the riſibility of a financeer. The deeper projects of modern policy
are

are of a very different nature: they confift in melting down the vigour of a nation by private and public corruption, tolerating every fpecies of abufe, invading the people's property by intolerable taxes, and under that pretence fubjecting the moft innocent and indifferent actions to reftraint. Wars of the moft deftructive nature are entered upon for every purpofe but that of national utility; and peace itfelf brings no alleviation of public burthens, nor always prevents their accumulation. At length, unnerved and harraffed, entangled on every fide with the inextricable well of debts, taxes, and penal laws, as well as infected with the fecret venom of all-pervading influence, a brave and generous people refign all claim to privileges it has long difufed, forgets that ever it was free, and finks into the eternal fleep of fervitude.

And fo univerfal have been thefe arts, fo general their fuccefs, that when we contemplate the different regions of the globe, we fhall find they have almoft all in turn become the victims of avarice and ambition. Afia has been the feat of immemorial tyranny; Africa fees all its coafts depopulated to fatisfy the demand of Chriftian luxury for flaves; Europe itfelf is on the point of yielding to the common deftiny. Government, that partial benefit, but univerfal evil, becomes, even from the moment of its inftitution, the engine by which

which the interests of the many are submitted to the caprices of the few. But moderate at first in its pretensions, and fearful of exciting too powerful an odium, it veils its baneful innovations under the semblance of order, public safety, and national defence. At length, like a stream, which flowing through an immense extent, has been gradually swelled into a torrent, by the recession of a thousand rivulets, it rises over every barrier, and deluges all, with irresistible fury. Mankind have then no other choice, but to worship the idols of their own creation, or to be exterminated by the sword which they have foolishly trusted to other hands. From that instant, there are no bounds to insolence on one side, or degradation on the other. The noblest empires seem only created for the sport and riot of a few conceited families; all the productions of the earth are monopolized; the elements themselves become subject to human pride; and man that believes himself the lord of all, is the only animal that starves amidst universal plenty.

This is the progress of every government; and however retarded in its course, it as invariably tends to despotism as rivers seek the sea by the laws of gravitation. Can any generous or humane mind, therefore, that is convinced of this truth, behold with disapprobation the struggles which are made in any corner of the globe for liberty.

liberty. Will he not wish to see the spoilers of the world, the enemies of common happiness, checked in their course, and new asylums opened to the suffering part of the species? But should the contest happen in the very country of which he is a member, will not a much more powerful motive intervene, his own immediate interest; at least if he has learned to attach other ideas to the term than that of personal ease or safety, or the wish to share the plunder, and riot in the spoils of others?

It is upon these motives that I confess I have uniformly detested the American war. No example could arise from the subjugation of that country, excepting a repetition of the common cruelties, which under the name of justice or policy are practised in all conquered countries; and particularly in those where public violence is stimulated and executed by civil animosity. The least that could have been expected, would have been executions, banishment, confiscations of property, and the establishment of a military government to extinguish every spark of liberty before it should begin to flame. I cannot pretend to assign the limits of ministerial mercy, but those that begin by invading every acknowledged right, and demolishing every public barrier, will rarely end by replacing them. On the contrary, the success of the United States affords an awful spectacle, which cannot

cannot be too often renewed for the inftruction of mankind, and the information of fovereigns. It teaches the poffeffors of power, to ufe that power with moderation, unlefs they would incur the hazard of lofing what is fo dear to their ambition. It teaches mankind at large, that neither the vaunted prowefs of mercenary armies, the poffeffion of unequalled riches, fleets that command the ocean, or all the refources of eftablifhed authority, are fufficient to prevail over minds that have once determined to meet death rather than fubmit to flavery. Above all, the eftablifhment of fo many free ftates upon the pureft principles of civil and religious liberty, affords the moft confolatory profpects to every friend of humanity. The fame fpirit which has directed their foundations may ftill extend their limits, till the immenfe continent of America become the feat of happinefs and population, and the refuge of all the miferable, from European tyranny. How different is this view of things from that which the narrow fchemes of felfifh policy would have prefented! That policy which rather than emancipate mankind wifhed to wage war with Providence, and ftop the courfe of nature; to defolate the nobleft portion of the univerfe, and rather make it the receptacle of noxious reptiles and beafts of prey, than fuffer it to be inhabited by men that dare to

think

think for themselves, and defend the privileges of their existence.

These were the general principles upon which I always reprobated the American war; but when I considered its probable consequences upon the safety and happiness of this country, motives of private interest concurred to augment my just abhorrence. It was too evidently begun upon principles which had no connection with public utility, however the public credulity might be ensnared to suffer its continuance. The interest of every people consists in a due administration of the laws which defend their persons and their property, in a plenty of those things which the sustenance of life requires, and in a freedom from those restraints and impositions which have so baneful an effect on commerce and agriculture in other parts of the world. Could any thinking man believe, that these salutary ends would be promoted by the desolation of America and the destruction of its inhabitants?—Those gentlemen and merchants who assented to the measure, with the laudable intention of lowering their taxes, and encreasing their markets, must explain their own ideas: to me it always appeared evident, that war could neither promote our commerce, nor diminish our burthens. Could the burning of towns, and the destroying every species of property, increase the American demand for British commodities, or contribute to the employment of our manufacturers? As much as the extinction of liberty in America, and the establishment of a military government there, would have tended to preserve our rights at home, and diffuse the blessings of the English constitution.

But every thing that the opposers of that disastrous war predicted at its commencement, has since been fatally accomplished. Our burthens, instead of being diminished, are increased to that enormous magnitude which threatens the annihilation of commerce and agriculture. The neighbouring nations of Europe, instead of viewing with indifference or applause the chastisement of our rebellious colonies, have ranged themselves on their side, as was foretold; and whatever may have been the original strength of the Americans, they have been so well supported by our ancient enemies and rivals, as to baffle all our past, and to be secure from all our future attempts. Instead of that contribution, which was the avowed object of the war, we have lost the monopoly of their commerce, and must become, if we wish to regain any part of it, suppliants to those whom we disdained to acknowledge as our equals. More than an hundred millions have been already squandered without the reduction of a single province; and more taxes imposed on national industry than I will venture to say, the exertion of ministerial

sterial œconomy will deliver us from in the ensuing century; though it should uniformly proceed in the same rapid torrent with which it has begun.

In the midst of these distresses, a gleam of hope breaks forth, if we deign to profit by our past miscarriages, and to learn wisdom from misfortune. Our late successes will facilitate the means of peace, if we are seriously inclined to propose or accept the terms which are adapted to our situation. Our enemies wearied with the ravages and losses of a doubtful war, will easily consent to breathe from their toils; the Americans will gladly return to their former peaceable occupations; and all Europe will lose its jealousy of a nation, that even in the midst of victory can resign the spirit of conquest.

But perhaps the measure of our calamities is not yet full, and the pride and folly which have so long opposed our happiness, may demand severer expiations than any we have yet offered. Our late successes, indecisive as they are, and inadequate to any other objects than the acquisition of peace, may raise new dreams of conquest, and renew the general infatuation. A people long accustomed to be deceived, too proud to yield, too indolent to reflect, too corrupted to be just or humane, may insist on kindling again the flames of war, and deluging the earth with blood. A minute nifter felfifh and interefted like his predeceffors, may feel more attachment to pomp and power than to the effential interefts of his country; with boundlefs ambition, but a contracted heart, he may take advantage of popular delufions to violate his own profeffions; or yielding to that mighty influence againft which he has fo long declaimed, may fteer the public veffel towards the very fhoals he has fo repeatedly pointed out, and inftead of making the port, feek for refuge amidft the ftorm.

In this cafe, I cannot expect to avoid the general fate, or to efcape that ruin againft which I have in vain endeavoured to warn my country. But amidft all the calamities which I forefee will burft upon us, it will be fome confolation to me, to have difcharged the duties of a virtuous citizen; and without intereft or ambition, without even the wifh or hope of fame, to have oppofed myfelf to the ftream of public prejudice, and enforced thofe falutary truths, upon which depend the fafety and happinefs of the people.

FINIS.

BOOKS printed for J. STOCKDALE, oppofite BURLINGTON-HOUSE, PICCADILLY.

1. AN ESSAY on CRIMES and PUNISHMENTS, with a View of and Commentary upon Beccaria, Rouffeau, Voltaire, Montefquieu, Fielding, and Blackftone. By M. DAWES, Efq. Price 4s. in Boards, 5s. bound.

2. An ADDRESS to the PEOPLE of the NETHERLANDS, on the prefent alarming and moft dangerous Situation of the REPUBLIC of HOLLAND; fhewing the true Motives of the moft unpardonable Delays of the Executive Power in putting the Republic into a proper State of Defence, and the Advantages of an Alliance with Holland, France, and America. By a Dutchman. Tranflated from the Dutch Original. Price 2s. 6d.

3. FACTS and their CONSEQUENCES: fubmitted to the Confideration of the Public at large; but more particularly to that of the FINANCE MINISTER, and of thofe who are, or mean to become, Creditors of the State. By JOHN, Earl of STAIR. Third Edition. Price 1s.

4. SUBSTANCE of the CHARGE of MISMANAGEMENT in his MAJESTY'S NAVAL AFFAIRS in the Year 1781, compared with the Authentic Papers laid before the Houfe on Mr. FOX's MOTION, in the Month of February, 1782. To which is added, A COMPLETE LIST of the DIVISION. Price 1s.

5. A Correct and Complete LIST of the MEMBERS who voted FOR and AGAINST the Hon. Mr. FOX's MOTION in the Houfe of Commons, on Wednefday the 26th of February, concerning the MISMANAGEMENT of the NAVAL DEPARTMENT. To which is fubjoined, An Alphabetical LIST of the ABSENTEES on that Occafion, with a few fhort Remarks annexed. Whereby is fhewn, beyond all Doubt, not merely what the Senfe of the Motion is, " but that there is, " at this Moment, a clear and decifive Majority of the Houfe " of Commons againft the prefent Conductors of public " Affairs." In Red and Black Characters. Price 2d. or 12s. per Hundred.

6. GENERAL CONWAY's MOTION for PEACE with AMERICA. In Red and Black Characters. Price 2d or 12s. per Hund.—A Correct and Complete List of the Glorious Majority on the Right Hon. General Conway's Motion for an Address to his Majesty, for the Purpose of procuring a Reconciliation with America, on Wednesday, February 27; as also Lists of the Minority and Absentees on that Occasion. To which are added, A few short Remarks on the Conduct, Conversation, and Connections, of several Members who voted with the Minister on that Evening, by Way of Supplement to the Red Book, by the Help and Comparison of which, it is humbly presumed, a pretty fair Account may be collected for so large a Minority on so popular a Question.

7. A LETTER from Mr. DAWES to JOHN HORNE TOOKE, Esq. occasioned by a Part of his Speech to the MIDDLESEX FREEHOLDERS, at HACKNEY, on the 29th of May, 1782. Price 1s.

www.ingramcontent.com/pod-product-compliance
Lightning Source LLC
Chambersburg PA
CBHW030907170426
43193CB00009BA/760